Trailer Sailing

A complete guide to choosing, handling, towing and living on board.

J C Winters

ADLARD COLES NAUTICAL
LONDON

First published by Adlard Coles Nautical 1994 an imprint
of A & C Black (Publishers) Ltd
35 Bedford Row, London WC1R 4JH

First edition 1994

ISBN 0–7136–3779–X

A CIP catalogue record for this book is available from the
British Library.

Typeset in Memphis 10/12pt by Falcon Graphic Art Ltd.,
Surrey.

Printed and bound in Great Britain by
The Cromwell Press, Melksham, Wiltshire

Contents

Introduction

Trailer sailing is for many people the ideal way for the owner and sailor of a small yacht to be totally independent and, in theory at least, to be unaffected by the petty tyrannies of boatyard or crane operator. With yacht and trailer hitched up behind the family car, the freedom of the open road as well as that of the open sea awaits. But are these freedoms only illusory, the very idea no more than another opportunity for designers and manufacturers of both yachts and trailers to create a need where previously none existed?

One cannot deny the delight of new sailing areas each weekend, of the possibility of family holidays in the Mediterranean and, on a more mundane level, the advantages of being able to store and lay up the boat conveniently in the security of your own garden. Some cynics, though, might argue that only the mentally challenged would willingly submit to the potential irritations arguably to be expected with trailer sailing: nightmare traffic jams, punctures, burnt-out wheel bearings, in addition to rigging and launching the yacht at the end of the overland journey. Not to mention the business of finding somewhere to store the trailer while you are at sea – nearly always with a daily rental fee to be paid – and taking all precautions necessary against possible theft.

Make no mistake – there are undoubtedly drawbacks. Towing a yacht on increasingly crowded roads can be quite daunting at times, as can manoeuvring on a steep and narrow slipway – especially when under the surveillance of a tail-back of like-minded mariners all impatiently waiting to launch or recover their own craft! And regulations must be complied with, a certain amount of paperwork completed and legal formalities observed.

But don't be deterred; attention to detail, conscientious route planning and experience gained gradually will smooth away all the doubts and problems which might assail a newcomer. The effort will prove well worthwhile and not only on the grounds of economics – although indisputably a well-chosen yacht with suitable trailer can offer an enthusiast considerable cost saving, particularly taking a long-term view. Even after making due allowance for the cost of the trailer, the increased petrol consumption when towing, and possible charges for use of a slipway, trailer sailing will certainly cost less than keeping a similar yacht in a marina berth (in most cases it will also be cheaper than a swinging mooring). This difference will be most appreciated by those who are denied the opportunity to sail as often as they would like: it makes little sense to fork out exorbitant sums of cash each year simply to keep the boat lying idle in its berth.

But even without the financial considerations, it is a pretty good way to approach cruising; once the knack of towing a trailer is mastered (and often the greatest hazard is that of simply forgetting that the beast is quietly and obediently following) overland journeys will become second nature, as will launching and rigging the boat in the minimum of time. The fascination of exploring new horizons is ever constant and areas of unspoilt coastline in Britain and abroad are within easy reach as they would not otherwise be to a small sailing cruiser whose overall speed is limited by the necessarily short waterline length.

Although it has long been common practice to trundle racing dinghies and the smaller one-design keel boats such as Flying Fifteens and Dragons around the countryside to Open Meetings, the operation used to be fraught with anxiety. Neither was it one to be embarked upon without a fair amount of spare cash handy in case of emergencies, since cars were not famous for reliability, nor trailers so well engineered. The boats were also vulnerable to damage imposed by the stresses of trailing; as befits racing craft they were quite lightly constructed of timber in the traditional fashion – fragile ribs with clinker or carvel planking which could dry out or split even when the vibration of the journey did not disturb the fastenings and cause seams and butt joints to spring adrift. It was not until the Second World War that wood-bonding glues were developed which proved suitable for marine use; by the late 1950s their use brought about a revolution in boat building. Designs of small sailing cruisers proliferated and these tiny but tough little ships sold in their thousands. Constructed in the main from sheet plywood, although a few types were of moulded veneer, these were really the first generation of trailer sailers, designed to be light enough to be towed by a family car – although it must be remembered that in those days a family car was something of a rarity! Any member of a yacht club unfortunate enough to be unmasked as the owner of such a vehicle could count on 'volunteering' to drive all the other members' boats, one by one, to distant regattas. Since the majority of these so-called 'pocket cruisers' (whose length ranged from 16 feet to around 22 feet overall) were encumbered by bilge keels as well as a centreline ballast stub and separate skeg-hung rudder, the fact that they actually engaged in competitive sailing might raise a few eyebrows today, but race they did and pretty aggressively too. That this hardy species were, in the hands of experienced crew, up to protracted coastal passages is borne out by the ambitious voyages completed – who has not heard of the exploits of *Shrimpy*, a 19-foot Caprice, typical of that era?

Thirty years on, a good number of these small ships are still in commission, a testament both to the construction materials and to the thoroughness of the builders. The march of progress, though, rather overtook them and, as true trailer sailers, with all the versatility that the term implies, the designs leave something to be desired.

Glassfibre and the increasing use of foam and balsa core construction allowed far better strength to weight ratios so that it became possible to tow larger boats behind smaller cars; at the same time considerable ingenuity was applied to methods of pivoting, swinging and lifting ballast keels. This permitted a second generation of efficient sailing yachts, typified by the E-boat, Sonata and Limbo, all of which were performance oriented and raced under the level rating rules or as active one-design classes. They effectively combined shallow draft for launching, were quick and simple to rig and lightweight to trail; furthermore (one test of a true trailer sailer this) they were blessed with accommodation which proved tenable either when cruising overland or sailing offshore.

And the third generation? Well, the 1990s are seeing considerable refinements in construction and design: hulls are lighter (and, manufacturers would claim, just as rugged) rigs are more efficient and the use of twin lifting keels and water ballast is proliferating. The choice is greatly expanded; it is indeed confusing as boat builders strive to create the perfect trailer sailer. The majority are pleasant and accommodating small craft which can provide a great deal of pleasure at very modest cost. Certainly there has never been more demand for good trailer sailers as mooring charges escalate. Regrettably, big business concerns are just becoming aware of public disenchantment and of a tendency to take to the road and, since these companies not infrequently monopolise access to slipways and foreshore, launching charges are also showing a tendency to rise.

But there still exist plenty of good public hards and some wonderful sailing areas to enjoy – and undeniably it is one of the most cost-effective options for those who really want to make the most of their sailing time. Hopefully, this book will help, not only when it comes to the choice of yacht and trailer (whether buying new or second-hand) but also in planning the holiday cruise. Some of the hints in handling and manouevring, both at sea and on land, may well also come in handy for the reader and transform trailer sailing into an enjoyable way of life.

1 Keel and Rudder

No matter how a yacht is designed – whether the end product is the result of computer-aided calculations, of freehand scribblings on the back of cigarette packets or the outcome of hours spent whittling at a chunk of yellow pine until a satisfactory hull shape emerges – the designer's art has always been regarded with a certain amount of awe.

Few skills are so dependent upon the interaction of as many variables as that of yacht design: the likely sailing area of the yacht must be considered, the number of crew, their strength and competence and the anticipated degree of domestic comfort below deck. Overall performance and predictable handling must be taken into account too. Aesthetics should be a factor, although these days it is often sacrificed to 'efficiency', which could be seen as merely an attempt to produce the most voluminous accommodation unit for a given waterline length. In the case of a small yacht (under 26 feet, which is about the maximum length for a viable trailer sailer), considerable skill is required to reconcile all these variables satisfactorily. The widespread use of calculator and computer is often blamed, perhaps rightly, for the resultant stereotypical designs, although, to be fair, the computing axiom of 'garbage in – garbage out' proves to be as true where yacht design is concerned as it is in any other field.

Stability

As variables exist so do constants, and the first of these is that hull speed is limited by waterline length; the only exception is in the case of a vessel designed to plane. Some 'cruising' sailboats with a waterline length of under 20 feet can indeed be induced to reach planing speeds, often in excess of 14 knots – although these would usually only be achieved in short bursts in very favourable conditions (and in the hands of a very hard-driving crew). Certainly such performance necessitates a rather extreme hull form coupled with ultra-light displacement – but then these are assets rather than liabilities so far as a trailer sailer is concerned! Less desirable may be the boat's highly-strung reactions to helm movement or sail trim: as a general rule, these performance-oriented boats may be, to put it mildly, less than docile, requiring a firm and knowledgeable hand on the tiller. Strategic positioning of the human ballast is also called for, indeed is often vital when sailing hard on the wind. This is because these small yachts, though very broad at deck level, tend to have a relatively narrow waterline beam and should be sailed upright for maximum efficiency (and to prevent the rudder stalling) so the crew may be sentenced to perch on the weather rail for the entire duration of a long haul to windward. This is not conducive to relaxed family cruising, and, especially in coastal waters, it could be argued that it is actually dangerous. In experienced hands, however, these boats can provide exhilarating sailing and share many of the characteristics of a large racing dinghy (including in severe conditions a propensity to knock-downs – although all are claimed to be self-righting and some to be unsinkable).

Lateral resistance

Leeway – or the means of preventing it – is another factor which is common to every vessel, power or sail alike. Sailing boats, with their slower speed through the water and the fact that winds have a habit of blowing straight from the intended destination rather than obligingly towards it, can never afford to ignore leeway, but even the largest power craft disregard its effects at their peril. Essentially it is caused by windage upon the hull, the superstructure and of course the rig itself, and is counteracted by the profile of the underbody – the deeper in relation to top hamper, the better. Once again, it is in the smaller yacht that the trade-off becomes more difficult – at least if the yacht is to offer any degree of functional accommodation below decks.

In the case of the majority of yachts, the keel not only provides lateral resistance, that is, the means of resisting leeway, but also stability and sail-carrying power. This means that the greater the weight of the keel in relation to the all-up weight of the yacht (the so-called ballast ratio) and the lower the centre of gravity, the more efficiently will the keel act as a lever arm so the greater the righting moment. Although stability is not the only criterion, it plays a large part in determining the amount of sail area a vessel can set, and up to what wind strengths it can still be carried to good purpose. This explains why racing yachts, especially nowadays, tend to have hulls closely resembling those of dinghies, with a deep but short fin keel.

Even disregarding the violent motion in a seaway engendered by the concentration of ballast within a small area, such an uncompromising approach is really only suitable for out-and-out racing craft as there are a number of other undesirable consequences of this kind of hull configuration – the first being that it is all too easy to run it aground! Approaches to harbours and most of the attractive creeks and anchorages tend to be on the shallow side (and there exists an unwritten law which dictates that the deepest keels encounter the foulest mud just a few moments *after* high water). In extreme cases, it can prove difficult to re-float the boat, as it will take the ground at a steep angle and the cockpit may fill before it lifts, so once firmly ensconced in the 'visitors' berth' the craft cannot possibly be left to its own devices, unattended on a rising tide.

Neither is beaching for a scrub any light matter; even drying out alongside scrubbing posts or a quay calls for care and attention as there is so little length of keel for the hull to rest on; the crew may have to stay ashore for the duration or at the very least, move around on deck with extreme caution – certainly any semblance of domestic life aboard would be ruled out! True, the light weight of these types for their overall length does mean, that they can be towed behind a relatively small car but the yard crane will be needed in order to launch (unless total immersion of the trailer is accepted and this is definitely not a thing to be undertaken lightly).

While the fixed fin scores highest on the efficiency scale, it is less attractive so far as any trailer sailing yacht is concerned, and in fact it would not be an exaggeration to state that it is a definite liability. But there are always going to be those to whom ruthless efficiency will supersede all other considerations (including that mundane one of running aground at the top of a spring tide and remaining there for an unexpectedly protracted holiday). It is with these buyers in mind that designers have concentrated their collective minds on ways of avoiding the bolting on of a large *fixed* chunk of ironmongery. Indeed, the search for the perfect compromise has been exercising them for at least fifty years. For there is no getting away from it: if it is windward ability, even windward ability at the expense of every other consideration, then a ballast fin with the maximum weight on the longest feasible lever arm is a points winner. So, therefore, said lever arm, complete with ballast must retract, fold or otherwise disappear within the hull in order to achieve this perfect compromise. It is hard to say whether these design variations are due to the popularity of these trailable boats or if the genus has evolved simply as a result of designers' efforts, but at any rate, in addition to the tried and trusty alternatives of bilge keel or centreplate, there are on the market today at least a dozen other options.

Having considered the fixed deep fin ballast keel, its drawbacks but also its superior efficiency for windward work at least, it comes as no great surprise that any method of combining effective lateral resistance and adequate ballast ratio with shallow draft is going to entail a compromise and, as usual in a smaller yacht, of less than 26 feet (9 metres) or so, there will have to be a careful trade-off between the hull proportions, keel or plate dimensions and in many cases, the internal accommodation.

Not all craft are dependent upon an external ballast keel to provide stability and lateral resistance: apart from motor vessels, working craft such as fishing smacks have relied to a great extent upon hull form stability, ie wide beam and deep underwater hull sections. Admittedly, there would be a type of keel on these boats, but this would merely be the long heavy timber which formed the external backbone of the vessel and did little to counteract leeway. Although yachts based on this type would have carried internal ballast either in the form of iron or lead pigs (or the engines themselves), fishing vessels, relied on the weight of the catch as ballast, though occasionally heaving a few sandbags aboard when leaving port. So they would not point to windward as well as a modern yacht, but on the whole this was not the object of the design, which was to reach the fishing grounds (often after negotiating shallow inshore waters which necessitated shoal draft), tow the nets and gear for just as long as was necessary, then race for home and the fish market. Of course, storms did rise without warning to veer or back unpredictably and this inability to claw to windward cost lives by the hundred and vessels by the score.

Internal ballast

Internal ballast on board yachts has long been regarded as messy, a potential cause of structural weakness and at best only moderately effective. Despite this, it has been in use since the earliest recorded times and it was not until the last century that it became common practice to fit an external ballast keel. Even then, bets were hedged and bilges crammed full of lead or iron pigs, and on occasion with an amalgam of scrap metal and concrete. However, internal ballast caused problems: the iron rusted and needed scaling and painting annually – and lead was very costly. If ingots were stowed loose they could break adrift in severe weather; if they were cast to fit between the frames, moving them for inspection was difficult, so neglect allowed wet rot to go undetected in the surrounding timber. Also the ballast took up space – which was always at a premium on a small vessel. Though stowed as low as possible in the bilges; it was still not low enough to exert any serious righting moment.

While the last two points rather count against internal ballast, in a glassfibre yacht, where a mixture of resin and metal pellets is integrally moulded into the bilge space, structural problems are eliminated; indeed the ballast mixture serves to further reinforce and strengthen the hull with the increased thickness offering additional protection against damage through a heavy accidental grounding. The ever-present fear that in the event of a knock-down (not by any means an unknown occurrence, even in sheltered waters) the ballast might shift with disastrous result, is also eliminated.

Water ballast is gaining in popularity nowadays. This is not surprising as it offers one very marked advantage over other forms of encapsulated ballast – that it can be dispensed with altogether for trailing or launching, thus reducing the all-up weight of the boat considerably. The water tank or tanks are simply filled and emptied by gravity: a valve is opened upon launching and the ballast compartment fills, then the valve is then shut off firmly. After sailing, with the boat on the trailer, the valve is opened once more, the water pours out and the unwanted trailing weight is promptly drained away!

The low-tech ballasting option is simply to chuck in bags of sand, shingle or pebbles. These may be either pre-filled and the bags carried within the hull while trailing (only to be laboriously removed when launching in order to decrease the draft) or, as is common practice, be filled with any material to hand at the launching site and stowed in place once the craft is safely afloat. Just so long as the containers do not puncture, this method serves well, particularly on smaller camping boats, though manhandling a half a dozen slippery

Fig 1

These types of keel/plate/movable ballast configurations are the ones most usually found but other combinations do exist, including the time-honoured ones of form stability (ie extreme beam) or movable human ballast.

a   Quadrant centreplate in conjunction with internal ballast (on very small boats the ballast may not be needed). The plate case takes up a good deal of room in the accommodation but the long plate, when lowered, aids directional stability. Off the wind, the plate may be partially lifted to reduce drag. On grounding, the plate can retract automatically and is unlikely to be damaged, though there is a tendency for the narrow slot to become packed solid with mud if the boat takes the ground regularly. In this sketch the plate is shown matched to a fixed, low-aspect rudder, not at its best when heeled but pretty well invulnerable to damage, though not to fair wear and tear!

c   Horizontally pivotting centreboard, unba lasted but with negative buoyancy (and not requiring a winch for raising) couple with internal water ballast. An increasing popular development for trailer sailers th as it makes possible a very low all-up tra ing weight once the ballast is drained (b the simple expedient of pulling the plug! and, plate up, the ability to float in only inches of water. Some reliance on form stability is essential as, obviously, the rig ing moment of the ballast is lessened by being relatively high up. Note that where water ballast tanks are moulded integral into a GRP hull, questions arise as to th quality and thickness of the gel coats; th tank could be a prime site for the onset unseen blistering.
In this sketch of a Macgregor 19 the ball and plate are backed up by twin low asp fixed rudders to provide the best directio control for this design, which has a dual purpose: sailing or planing with a mediu size outboard.

b   Centreplate contained entirely within the ballast stub keel. An excellent compromise which combines shallow draft, weight low down where it is most needed, deep draft for windward work – all these with an

acceptably shallow draft for trailing. Her too the centreplate is used with a fixed shallow rudder, although a deeper pivot blade might be more efficient.

Tandem keel with 'wings'. The wings help to keep the ballast concentrated low down and provide a stable base for the boat if it takes the ground. Since they are angled slightly downwards the wings immerse more deeply as the boat heels and so increase the effective draft. The length of the keel makes for good directional stability and an easy motion at sea, whilst the gap between the fore and aft keels ensures that the boat is not too ponderous when it comes to altering course! It has a moderate draft for trailing, launching and recovery, but it scores in this respect over a conventional fin without any great sacrifice in the way of pointing ability. It is generally partnered with a single fixed low aspect rudder, and sometimes twin rudders for greater efficiency when heeled.

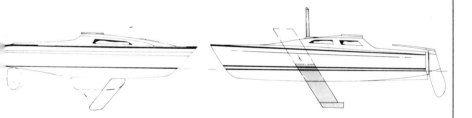

Horizontally pivotting (swinging) ballast keel. This type of keel, when lifted, remains outside the hull, virtually halving the draft. Efficient when fully lowered, this configuration permits shoal water sailing with the keel in intermediate positions. Since it contains the entire ballast, however, it calls for a powerful winch or hydraulic system (expensive) when raising and lowering. Here it is shown with an elliptical rudder which lifts vertically within a trunking. This method allows the rudder to be sited where gives the best directional control over a wide range of conditions and heel angles, but is rather vulnerable to damage. Neither can it be partially retracted for shallow water use – only lifted completely clear for sailing or a drying mooring.

f Lifting fin and bulb ballast keel. The keel in the sketch, having as it does a high aspect ratio, lifts clear through the deck/coachroof; others of less extreme form may reach only as far as the deckhead internally. The angled trunking takes up a good deal of room in the accommodation but the keel is very efficient once lowered, since the ballast is on the extreme lower end of a long lever arm. Retracted, only the ballast bulb remains outside the boat. It is possible to sail with the keel partially lifted without a dangerous loss of stability, though this would hardly be recommended practice. The keel is coupled in this sketch with a horizontally pivoting rudder blade which will kick up in the event of grounding.

continued

Fig 1 continued

g Lifting wing keel. Basically a more refined variant of the above. In this case, the keel is longer and so distributes the ballast more evenly along the boat which reduces the tendency to pitch associated with deep and narrow fins. The keel box will intrude into the saloon but can almost certainly be included within the galley space or form part of the saloon table mounting. As with a fin and bulb keel, a powerful winch or hydraulics will be necessary in order to raise and lower it. With the keel lifted, only the ballast wings remain outside the boat,

but these provide a stable and protective platform upon which the boat can be drie out. The lifting wing keel is shown here w a fixed only moderately shallow rudder which would negate the advantage of hav ing a lifting keel in the first place – but thi is not unknown especially in one-off designs. The partial skeg, also very com- mon, offers little protection to the rudder. Indeed rudders hung in this way are notably susceptible to damage in the low bearing and across the lower half of the blade.

h Vertically lifting ballast keel. Very popular indeed as this type takes up little cabin space, requires only a relatively simple lift- ing purchase and winch, and is very effi- cient when lowered. (It *must* be locked into position when lowered; some designs have no provision for doing this and securing bars and bolts should be fitted as a matter of priority.) If there is a negative aspect to the vertically lifting keel it is simply that it must be regarded as a fixture once lowered and the boat should not be sailed with it in an intermediate position. On the other hand, although the keel is narrow and short, it is possible to dry the boat out alongside on it as with a fixed fin. This type of keel is mostly combined with a vertically lifting rudder, a design which is strong, has a positive feel, and can function when partly raised. Such a rudder, though, is not, as a rule, designed to kick up on impact, though a shear pin can be incorporated in the aft edge of the rudder head.

i Unballasted bilge boards combined with moulded internal ballast. These boards make for deep draft, ideal when working windward, and they lose little efficiency a the boat heels. The boards do not intrude into the accommodation, although the tw cases are of course an added expense when considering building costs. They function best on a light dinghy type hull w a degree of form stability, as borne out b the ultra-light and very quick 'Red Fox'. T boards make possible a flush bottom and very shallow draft, and the boat can be sailed downwind effectively with one or both boards partly or entirely retracted. A deep vertically lifting rudder works well in combination with these bilge boards.

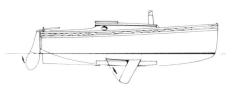

Fixed splayed ballasted bilge keels. These, at their best, can be hydrodynamically first class with low drag and efficient section. The slight angle of splay means that draft is increased as the angle of heel increases. They may give rise to structural problems where boats are left on a drying mooring; encapsulated integrally moulded keels suffer less but cannot easily be constructed with the outward splay. As is often the case, the boat is steered by a fixed low aspect rudder; if there is no skeg, there will be an inclination for the boat to sit on its tail when drying out.

Lifting ballasted bilge keels in conjunction with internal ballast. This is a very effective compromise for a trailer sailer: it allows a flush bottom, variable draft, and minimal intrusion into the cabin space. Though of metal, the keels are not weighty enough to require heavy winches and the internal ballast, though positioned higher than the optimum, ensures an easy motion under way. When used along with a horizontally pivoting rudder, this combination is excellent for exploring quiet shallow backwaters and creeks.

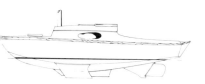

Twin bilge keels of steel plate coupled with a centreline ballast keel. This type, favoured in the sixties by many Robert Tucker designs is, on a small boat, arguably the worst of all combinations, since the draft is too shallow to point close to the wind and there is a massive clutter of resistance-inducing appendages on the underbody! That said, the construction is sturdy, the ballast provides good stability and, so long as sheer speed is not an objective, the configuration seems to suit many cruising boats and their owners. The rudder most widely favoured is a shallow fixed blade to a full skeg – tough as they come but all adding to the underwater drag!

sandbags may not add to the appeal of embarking upon a sailing holiday.

In a trailer sailer, once under way, it should be pointed out that no matter what form the internal ballast comes in, it should remain securely in place since it is not generally regarded as acceptable practice to hurl sandbags from side to side for extra leverage, however tempting this may be on a hard slog to windward! Neither is it recommended that the practice on racing skiffs of jettisoning ballast – or surplus crew members – for the downwind leg be adopted!

It can be seen that although internal ballast provides stability and sail-carrying power – albeit with a relatively high centre of gravity for which due allowance must be made in the hull form, whether in the type of section or in increased beam – in itself it provides little in the way of lateral resistance. Therefore a way has still to be found to counteract leeway yet also restrict the draft.

Centreplates

In a boat of traditional timber construction, it would have been usual for this compromise to be arrived at by the provision of a horizontally pivoting centreplate, usually of mild steel. This would be housed in an internal timber trunking. Not only did this long case obtrude into the accommodation, however, but it was time-consuming to construct, and since a slot had to be cut in the hog through which the plate operated, the structure of the vessel was weakened. Due to the incessant flexing of the plate, stresses on the case inevitably led to movement in fastenings: this resulted in leakage and, almost inevitably, to localised rot. Even on a 20-footer the plate would be relatively heavy – in excess of 100 lb (45 kg) – and probably need a winch to raise it. And of course the pivot bolt required constant inspection and regular replacement. But there was, and still is, one plus with a horizontally lifting plate: on grounding (or inadvertently coming into direct conflict with an underwater object) the plate kicks up safely, automatically retracting into the case and so, usually, avoiding serious damage to the hull.

Although the advantage is marginal, especially in a heavier yacht not designed for sheer speed, any retractable plate or board may, if partially raised, give a lift when sailing downwind as drag will then be reduced. There is, however, less lateral area to counteract any tendency to roll, and with less grip forward there could also be a loss of control should the yacht have to harden up into the wind unexpectedly without the time to drop the plate.

Accepting that the main arguments against centreplates are those of construction and a relatively high centre of gravity where a light boat with a degree of form stability is concerned (and most modern purpose-designed trailer sailers are variants on this theme), provided that there is sufficient internal ballast, the configuration is eminently practical. If there is a drawback it is in a barely measurable diminution of ability to stand up to the full sail area on the wind in a stiff breeze.

This is arguably exacerbated by today's trend towards the use of boards for centreplates rather than the heavier steel plates. These boards, usually constructed of timber, sheathed with GRP or laminated from it, incorporate just sufficient ballast to provide negative buoyancy: they sink of their own volition once the retaining line is released but are still light enough to be raised without a winch, even by a youngster. Any slight loss of righting moment associated with the use of a board would hopefully be compensated for in hull and rig design.

Unless it is possible to contain the centreplate casing completely within the ballast with the plate operating through it, as a narrow, deep foil or an L-shaped plate usually can, its intrusive presence within the accommodation area will have to be either tolerated or disguised. With space so much at a premium, especially in boats under 20 feet in overall length, neither option is easy. Whether the case forms part of the galley unit, or as is more usual, serves as the base for a fixed saloon table, movement and leg room in the vicinity will be rather restricted – but then the design of a small boat is invariably a constant compromise between living space and efficient performance.

In a modern yacht laminated in GRP or, given today's highly sophisticated glue and resin composites, constructed of timber, problems with the structure can be virtually discounted. The case may be integrally moulded with the hull or, when constructed of wood, be so well braced and sealed that it should withstand all wringing strains without difficulty, so there will be no problems with leaks and seepage leading to the eventual deterioration of the adjacent hull.

Bilgeboards

If a single board or plate is efficient, is it then reasonable to suppose that two will be doubly effective? There is a school of thought which maintains that this is definitely the case, and not entirely without good reason.

There is nothing new in twin lifting bilge boards (or plates or keels, for that matter). In truth, few ideas in the world of yachting can claim to be totally innovative. All that is truly new is the technology of today: this has made it feasible to put into practice many design ideas which would formerly have been considered outrageous – though some racing craft built at the turn of the century would, even now, raise a few eyebrows!

Although many of the racing boats built forty years ago have deteriorated beyond all hope of repair, some of the cruisers are still very much alive and sailing. One of the more unorthodox of these, though perhaps not the best known, is the 26 foot Fairey Atlanta. This bulky but remarkably light-weight centre cockpit sloop, constructed of hot moulded veneer, was specifically designed in the early sixties to be towed by a family car. With its twin ballast keels retracted, it had little more draft than a largish racing dinghy. On the wind, with the twin keels fully lowered, it performed acceptably rather than exuberantly but, off the wind, it was quick and docile, the soft sectioned hull lent excellent directional stability by those keels. Pretty it most certainly wasn't; the Atlanta with its heavily rolled side decks and blister coachroof looks distinctly cumbersome when compared with today's stylish yachts of similar size and, it must be admitted, superior performance and accommodation. Nor was the Atlanta's accommodation greatly enhanced by the quantity of exposed pipework, pumps and valves of the hydraulic lifting keel system (used in some examples) festooned around the main cabin! But the boat was undoubtedly way ahead of its time and has now achieved 'classic' status.

One point in favour of twin board systems is simply that the draft – and therefore the amount of lateral resistance – is increased slightly as the boat heels. If the boards have a degree of outward splay rather than being designed parallel to the waterline, this characteristic is more pronounced. Equally, if the boards are splayed the weather board will be brought closer to the horizontal and, when ballasted, will

Twin bilge boards (shown here partially raised) coupled with a flush bottom, as in the Red Fox twenty footer, combine the advantages of shallow draft for trailing and launching, excellent lateral resistance once they are lowered, and minimal intrusion into the living space.

exert an increased righting moment.

The second argument in favour of twin boards is significant too. In the restricted available space aboard a small yacht the boards, whether they lift in the horizontal or vertical plane, occupy very little space. If they do lift vertically, it is common for them to project through the side decks in the raised position, although they can, of course, be lifted completely clear if required.

And last but not least is the fact that any form of lifting keel or board can be immediately raised if the boat is unlucky enough to run aground. However, if grounding or, worse, leaving the boat on a half-tide mooring, beware the accumulation of mud and sand which builds up within the slots, sets to the consistency of concrete and has been known to immobilise everything totally!

Bilge keels

Fixed bilge keels, still perhaps the most usual compromise between sailing ability and light draft, are especially suited for yachts intended to take the ground, whether on a regular basis or just from time to time, perhaps when creek-creeping. The twin keels provide a level base on which to dry out, remain stable even on rough tide-scoured banks, and keep the underbody clear of any odd small rocks or debris. Admittedly they automatically entail an increase in draft, not to mention a small penalty exacted in the form of increased drag, but balanced against these factors is the simplicity and ruggedness of construction.

Not that the design of bilge keels is altogether straightforward; there is considerable disagreement amongst designers and owners as to the best form they should take. For that matter, there is also the vexed question of whether bilge keels should merely be responsible for lateral resistance or, in addition, provide the righting moment. Modern thinking tends towards the latter idea, although this could be due simply to the fact that, with a glassfibre yacht, it is easy to encapsulate the necessary ballast within a keel integrally moulded with the hull.

The post-war generation of plywood pocket cruisers usually settled for the first option, that of twin keels fabricated from steel plate and bolted by a flange through the hull to an integral bilge stringer, the actual stability of the boat being imparted by a short centreline ballast stub some ten inches or so in depth. Unfortunately this was far too shallow to be very effective. The bilge keels were almost always given an outward splay allowing a trailing draft of 18 in or so in the case of an 18-footer, but once heeled the draft increased and the lateral resistance was quite reasonable. Drag, however, was not. This was the real bugbear of this kind of configuration, all the more pronounced in boats of such diminutive size, boats which in any case, added further to their problems by hanging a separate rudder to a full aft skeg. As a type, these cruisers were hydro-dynamic bumble-bees: however, like the bumble-bee itself, they remained blissfully unaware of their theoretical inability to function and sailed on regardless, giving their owners a lot of pleasure – just so long as progress to windward was not timed by a stopwatch.

The modern hydrofoil section ballast bilge keel configuration has largely superseded that of the plate and centreline ballast, although these are still to be found on displacement cruising craft. The ballasted bilge keels are deep enough to provide adequate lateral resistance and without any inconvenient bits of cast iron appended amidships, the wetted surface – and so therefore drag – is kept to a minimum.

In fairness, it must be admitted that no bilge-keeler will ever knife to windward as decisively as her deep-fin sister with efficient keels, though it is unlikely that the crew, except when racing, would notice much difference. In a cruising boat the reduction in downwind rolling, which is a characteristic of bilge-keelers, should more than outweigh any small loss on the wind; the majority of these boats, even with the wind right aft, steer as though on rails. However, by the same token, don't expect them to spin like a top on command: however refined the keel design, there is still some extra underwater resistance. In an effort to cut this down, designers did experiment with slots cut through each keel but on the whole, this only served to increase turbulence – and, of course, expense.

. With the righting ballast contained within the keels, the further the boat heels the greater the leverage exerted by the weather keel as it approaches the horizontal. There is, though, the valid counter argument that while the weather keel is doing its best to keep the boat upright, the lee keel is doing its utmost to pull the hull deeper into the water and increase the angle of heel! Efficiency is improved where the keels are designed with ten degrees or so of outward splay. Such keels may be constructed of cast iron, through bolted to the hull or attached with studs, but they are often moulded as separate entities, through fastened to an internal girder and subsequently bonded to the GRP hull.

Splayed keels are inclined to give rise to structural problems if the yacht is constantly left on an exposed half-tide mooring. In such a situation the entire weight of the hull is brought to bear directly upon the keel, often after half an hour or so of pounding on an unyielding surface – and sand or mud under compression can be as hard as steel. This pressure forces the keels to splay further over a period of time, and eventually wrenches the fastenings. Since it is generally necessary to cut through part of the internal mouldings and furniture in order to put matters to rights, re-fastening may be quite costly, though it is becoming a pretty routine operation.

Some classes – such as the Snapdragon – have bilge keels squarely set at right angles to the waterline; these are moulded integrally with the hull, the hollow keel afterwards being filled with ballast and sealed. Not perhaps the most strictly sophisticated in form (and rather inclined to slam heavily when working hard to windward) these keels do have one major advantage: the cost factor. It is cheaper and quicker by far to mould the hull and keels in one piece (and of course splayed keels would prevent the hull's release from its mould). A second favourable point is the trouble-free structure. Apart from erosion of the lower edge of the keel where the boat takes to the ground regularly – and this can be easily put right without recourse to professional help – problems are rarely encountered.

The lifting keel

Possibly it is the lifting ballast keel which is most closely associated with the specialised trailer sailer. Terminology is a bit imprecise here because, strictly speaking, a lifting keel is raised vertically like a daggerboard and a swing keel pivots horizontally, although the terms do seem to be used rather indiscriminately.

Both systems have much to be said for them; the major differences lie in the details. The righting ballast is just where it is needed, low down. The boat with keel raised will have a completely flush bottom and minimal draft. Where the keel is raised vertically, the trunking will be compact and not make dramatic inroads upon accommodation (although, with the keel raised for trailing it reaches the deckhead and it must be accepted that those living on board will find its presence somewhat intrusive). But then there is no aspect of yacht

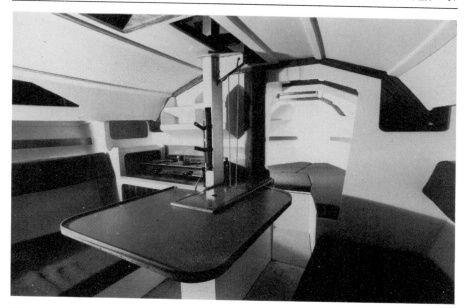

The interior of the lift-keel eighteen foot Mirador showing how the keel box is incorporated into the accommodation. The jockey winch for lifting the keel can be seen in the mast support pillar.

design without its down side; every argument in favour of one system will generate a chorus of objections. One misapprehension connected with lift-keelers is that the entire weight of the keel is suspended by a thread – or more accurately by a wire. It isn't, of course, and on no account should it be (except while being raised or lowered). That said, there were one or two exceptions, and it is to be fervently hoped that these have all now been modified and made safe.

Whether or not it was the first, the 22-foot E-boat was probably the best-known lifting keel boat; a very successful one-design raced and cruised all over Europe and with a very active class association. Responsive enough to race enjoyably either under level rating rules or in club handicap events, this flush-decked trailer sailer proved to be quite tractable, even in inexperienced hands. The ingenuity of the keel lift system plays a major part in this boat's success story: once the keel is lowered and locked into position, the boat is apparently transformed into a fixed-keeler capable of being dried out alongside, standing on the keel (although personally I never risked it as the bottom of the keel seems a bit too short to provide a secure touchdown point). The bolt-locking method is, in essence, quite simple to operate and only takes a few minutes.

Lifting keels do of course have to be lifted – this entails a wire, purchase and a winch: in the case of the E-boat, a small jockey winch mounted on the deckhead, demountable when not in use. Only minimal physical effort is involved in raising the keel (well within the capability of a youngster) and the entire process normally takes about four minutes (although an unplanned grounding on a falling tide seems to concentrate the actions wonderfully and I have managed it in half that time!). Other designs use a conventional ratchet winch and wire, equally effective so long as the cable is regularly checked for kinks or damaged strands.

Although some E-boat sailors have made up sets of shorter locking bolts so as to sail with slightly reduced draft on shallow and sheltered Continental lakes, this practice owes more to expediency than seamanship, and no lift-keeler should be sailed in tidal waters without the keel locked firmly down to its fullest extent since, once raised, the centre of gravity is raised with it and becomes dangerously high.

There is a school of thought maintaining that the inability (or, more accurately, inadvisability) to reduce draft under way gives a centreplate yacht a margin of safety over a lift-keeler (or for that matter, a fixed-fin keeler). It is held that in survival conditions offshore, when lying a'hull (in other words, with hatches battened down and the yacht left to her own devices) that once the plate is up, a centreplate boat will simply sideslip – going harmlessly with the wave action rather than resisting it – and thereby decrease the risk of being rolled. There may well be some truth in this, since when sailing myself at sea in strong winds in a Finn dinghy where a capsize seemed, to put it mildly, undesirable, lifting the plate in squalls and allowing the boat to blow to leeward safely was my standard operating procedure, and one which always got me home safely.

One thing which should be borne in mind with certain types of lift keel (and centreplate) yachts is the possibility that if anchored or moored in an exposed site, extreme weather conditions may result in water slopping through the case or trunking: this may gradually inundate the boat and cause it to founder. Such a thing actually happened to two lift-keelers on my home moorings during the storm of 1987 – and suggests that some means of retaining a secure seal on the keel or plate box top is essential.

A swing or pivoting keel may either be retracted completely within the hull or, once lifted, take up position outside,
flush against the hull. This latter option is not at all a bad
compromise between shoal draft for ditch crawling or creeping home on the last of the tide (when the boat can safely be
sailed with the keel lifted as even then the centre of gravity
remains within safety limits) and deep draft for serious sailing, with an unobstructed interior either way. Draft will
always be deeper than for a flush-bottomed boat of similar
length but this, even when launching, should be a minor
inconvenience.

Where a swing keel is housed within the hull, the only
minor irritation is that of the space the case occupies – and, as
with any other type of weighty ballast keel, the siting of the
lifting gear, whether this be hydraulic, winch or screw jack.

This hardly exhausts the list of variants on the theme:
amongst other designs are a retractable fin and bulb keel, lifting wing keels and both bilge and centreplates retracting into
ballast keels. Each type or combination of types has pros and
cons – and some are more suitable for some types of sailing
than others. For a trailer sailer the priorities are of course
going to be shoal draft, maximum accommodation compatible with overall length, and preferably, simplicity of operation and maintenance.

Rudders

What holds true for the keel also, to a great extent, holds true
for the rudder, another fruitful source of headaches for the
designer. In theory, the type of keel determines the type of
rudder or rudders, as designers seek ever more complicated
answers to the question. In practice there are some curious
anomalies.

Just how well the rudder performs depends not only upon
blade area and depth but also its suitability to the length,
beam and section of the hull which it is to steer. This may
seem to be stating the obvious but, in all too many cases, the
design of the rudder seems literally to be an afterthought –
this both from the point of view of efficiency and of excessive
vulnerability to damage.

In the case of any boat with variable draft, where it may
not be protected by a skeg, or to a lesser degree by the keel or
keels, the rudder blade must be capable of lifting clear should

it foul any underwater obstruction; in a trailer sailer it is clearly helpful if it can either be raised, or removed completely, for launching, recovery and when possible, trailing.

The majority of lift-keel or centreplate craft, particularly those in the smaller size bracket, simply hang the rudder on the transom; here it is quick to lift off when required, can easily be designed to be raised clear of the water on demand and, last but not least, exerts the maximum pressure for the minimum tiller movement. The latter is quite important for a racing boat as excessive see-sawing at the helm has a braking effect. But a transom-hung rudder on an excessively beamy yacht, especially one with the beam carried well aft (the so-called 'wedge of cheddar' type) is a recipe for disaffection if not disaster. The angle of heel increases when sailing hard, causing the rudder to be lifted clear of the water leaving the boat to gripe uncontrollably up into the wind. Coping with this may be an acceptable risk when racing but is certainly not so when cruising with the family, especially in crowded waters. A rudder which is underhung and set inboard from the transom, will give more positive control in lively going but, no matter however advantageous this is from the handling aspect, it is difficult to combine with an ability to retract. The best compromise seems to be that of incorporating blade and stock as a single unit within a frame which lifts completely through a daggerboard-type slot as it did with the Evolution 24. Here, the rudder can be removed as necessary but cannot be operated in any intermediate position – which precludes any ideas about creek-creeping! Perhaps more important is the fact that such a rudder is poorly engineered to cope with possible impact; indeed, it may well be forced partially into the slot and jam immovably.

Twin rudders, although less revolutionary than manufacturers would have us believe (dual systems have been in existence for at least a century, probably far longer), are claimed to prevent loss of bite when the boat is sailing on her ear. To my own way of thinking, fixed twin rudders, especially when unprotected by skegs, combine the worst of all worlds – extra drag, more components to break, twist or otherwise suffer damage when running aground (or worse, if being accidentally forced to dry out) and all for very little real gain. Even if twin transom-hung rudders, as on the Beneteau 601, smack of a design gimmick, there is at least a degree of inherent logic: the boat is beamy and the pair of rudders could well improve both heeled and downwind steering.

The twin fixed rudders of the Beneteau 601, allowing the outboard to be mounted on the centreline. These rudders play outwards for added efficiency when heeled.

There must be slight concern about damage since the blades are fixed but they do not project below the depth of the lifting keel when it is in the raised position against the underbody (and they are, at least, instantly accessible for repair should it ever become necessary). There is also a plus in that they allow an outboard to be mounted on the centreline where it will not obstruct the action of the tiller.

It was usually the case that the rudder blade was designed to lift in the same plane as the keel. Nowadays this precept has been largely abandoned for rudders whose blades are raised vertically through a substantial steel or timber head. Apart from the vexed question of susceptibility (which would emerge victorious should there be a close encounter with a rock?) this method is preferable, at least for those who value a positive feel to the helm. However well constructed in the first place, a horizontally lifting rudder is always subject to wear on the pivot bolt and, in any case, the bearing area of the cheek is insufficient to retain the blade firmly in position: there are few things more unsettling to a helmsman than feeling the rudder wiggling like a loose tooth.

Leaving aside any worries about precision of handling, it is worth pointing out that there are few portions of a yacht's vital anatomy so prone to depredation as the rudder, and that's without taking into account the effect of impact or grounding upon its structure. Solid timber rots, especially around metal fittings or fastenings, plywood delaminates, and mild steel corrodes. Glassfibre is not without its problems either, especially in rudders with an integrally moulded stainless steel sock or armature. Potential trouble sources in wood or metal are usually fairly obvious; in the case of a glassfibre rudder any deterioration gets under way from within and cannot initially be seen, although the process may be assumed if there are any signs of rust weeping through the gel (a clear sign that the encapsulated stock is corroding). More obvious will be splits along the leading and trailing edges. Any rudder can be easily knocked out of alignment, whether during the course of sailing or launching, but spade rudders are perhaps the most liable to suffer this. The stock may bend and the blade then 'bind' against the hull, and possibly jam, if the helmsman has used brute force on the helm. It is always sensible to check for full and free movement of the steering before setting off, and it goes without saying that pintles and gudgeons should be examined for damage or strain. Don't overlook the rudder retaining pin if one is fitted, and all control lines. Rudder failure is a common cause of acute embarrassment; given searoom it is not too difficult to rig up a jury steering system (even a bucket from the quarter will give a measure of directional control) but in confined waters, the consequences can be serious, and expensive!

$1.500 \ kg \ or$

$\times \ 2.205 = 3307.5 \ lb$

BROWNS BOOKS

*Booksellers, Stationers, H.M.S.O. and Ordnance Survey Agents
Library and Educational Suppliers*

With Compliments

22-28 GEORGE STREET, HULL, HU1 3AP
TELEPHONE: (0482) 25413. FAX: (0482) 227705

2 Design of the Hull

Of course, there is rather more to the design of the hull than simply ensuring that it will float and, hopefully, proceed in the general direction requested by the helmsman! The designer must calculate not only the stability and lateral resistance but also somehow impart that elusive quality known as sea-kindliness. Because a dedicated trailer sailer is necessarily a complex beast, it calls for a careful balance of qualities which could be regarded as mutually incompatible: to wit, acceptable windward performance, downwind control, and the ability to heave-to if necessary. These attributes are essential to any cruising boat worthy of the name, since no vessel which ever put out to sea could guarantee immunity to calm or gale. However, in smaller craft these aspects are very difficult to reconcile with the domestic requirements of the crew, and where the great selling point of any design is the number of berths which can be wedged into a given overall length, obviously something has to suffer.

Each individual will have established a list of requirements when considering the purchase of a trailer sailer. Quite often it will be the keel configuration which is the decisive factor. To one owner, bent on serious racing, it may be quite acceptable regularly to dunk a deep fin-keeler and either await the tide or pay through the nose for crane or hoist at the end of a race; to another skipper whose aim is relaxed family cruises around the coastline, the hassle inseparable from a deep draft boat would be a calamitous waste of sailing hours. Those who contemplate leaving the boat on drying moorings for any length of time may be happier with a bilge-keeler, whilst dedicated gunk holers, of whom there are many, might do best with a swing keel or centreplate yacht whose draft can be varied under way. So, although the keel type might not be the primary concern for the owner of larger, displacement cruising yacht, it is probably fair to say that it does play a large part in the selection of a trailer sailer.

This book is mainly concerned with craft between 16 and 26 feet in length, although the 15-foot West Wight Potter has become almost a cult boat and there is even an eight-foot long single berth cruiserette, cheerfully bracketed as a trailer

A twenty foot Beneteau 601 on the slipway – note the swing keel nestling against the underbody. On a ramp as steep as this, it would be good practice to chock the wheels before leaving the car! The steepness of this slipway also suggests that it might be wisest to remove the rudders as they could be damaged if the boat tilts even slightly.

sailer! It is fair to say that, on the whole, the craft tend to conform to a basic overall pattern, one that is forced upon them by the designer's brief: a high-volume hull with fine entry and broad flat run aft, very similar to that of a racing dinghy; the keel or keels being separate from the hull rather than faired into the turn of the bilge, as in the classic type of deep keel 'traditional' yacht. In the majority of cases the freeboard will be high in order to provide an illusion of creature comfort below decks; in the case of the smaller types, below 20 feet or so, it will almost certainly be too high to be aesthetically pleasing – although colour-coded strips and graphics are considered to minimise this slab-sidedness.

Design and handling

But though such image enhancements may help, they canno

put the proverbial quart into a pint pot – all they can do is disguise the size of the container! It seems strange that, except in the case of the highly competitive state-of-the-art racing yacht, few people question the design of a small yacht or the claims which may be made for it.

While the overall performance of any vessel is dependent to some extent upon the skill and seamanship of the crew, a small, light, displacement yacht places far more emphasis upon the ability and, in adverse weather, the sheer stamina of its crew members than its larger sister. Well sailed smaller yachts are capable of withstanding almost anything the sea can throw at them, but they have to be handled with a degree of care and forethought; they should always be reefed before being overpowered in gusts and not allowed to heel excessively, especially in close quarters where stalling of the rudder blade may cause loss of control and a possible collision. Under some combinations of sail, a light boat may be reluctant to come about, while certain designs with a shallow forefoot may come about but then fall off uncontrollably to leeward.

Inevitably the snappy, sometimes violent motion in a heavy sea is tiring for the crew. In the sort of wind strengths that make sailing a family pleasure rather an exercise in endurance, the majority of trailer sailers are pretty docile but there are some sportier ones which are over-sensitive to the distribution of crew weight. These, in anything over 18 knots or so of wind, need to be sailed with something of the concentration demanded by a racing dinghy with sheets and traveller played constantly. This is fine if the boat has been purchased with that knowledge in mind, but it can be disastrous if the fact is discovered when caught in half a gale with a family crew. To a youngster scrabbling for a foothold on the weather side of a sharply-heeled beamy boat, that seven-foot drop into the water takes on the nature of a descent into an abyss – and to be honest, a good many adults would also find it unsettling.

But trailer sailers are very attractive to the first-time buyer; they are priced to appeal, usually look quite good, they are unquestionably versatile and they are invariably put across as being a doddle for even a novice to sail. Frankly some are, some not. But just how is a buyer to differentiate?

There is nothing like experience, so ask other owners. Get information from the Class Association if there is one. Naturally, there will be bias, but less than from those who market and sell the boats! If you can wangle a trial sail, all to the good, especially if conditions are boisterous!

If advice is not forthcoming – and even if it is – a basic understanding of hull design should give you a reasonable idea of just how the boat will behave – and why. It will, a least, make it possible to weed out those boats, few though they are, that have characteristics, for one reason or another so exaggerated as to make the boat intractable, possibly unmanageable.

Lines and shape

It used to be more common than it is today for the lines drawings of yachts to be published. In these drawings, the sections, waterlines and buttock lines give an accurate three-dimensional view of the projected hull. Presumably, this diffidence now is to prevent anonymous persons of dubious honesty tracing the lines and producing spurious copies of the boat in some backyard (which would be pretty well impossible as anyone attempting to scale up to full size from such small published drawings would soon realise!).

A yacht's shape is made up of curves, and it is these which are expressed in the lines drawing. The sections are transverse slices through the hull, measured at certain fixed points known as the stations. Those lines which cut through fore and aft parallel with the flotation line are known as the waterlines, and the lines produced vertically fore and aft are the buttocks. The diagonals, which can be seen through the sections, indicate the heeled shape of the boat and are also used for fairing in when the drawings are brought up to full size. On looking at the plan, it can easily be seen that the waterlines indicate the wave-making effect of the upright hull while the buttock lines show the section, every line being interrelated. Interpreting the lines plan is not unlike reading a contour map: the closer the lines on any given plane, the sharper the curvature of that area.

It is the fore and aft plane of the hull, the section on the load waterline, which decides wave-making characteristics and therefore the motion and speed of the boat, although this latter, in a displacement boat, is also determined by the length of the immersed waterline. The type of waterline associated with smacks and working boats had a noticeably blunt entry and a finer, rather drawn-out run aft. This was efficient when the vessel sailed upright in light to medium airs but

Fig 2 Lines perspective.

Sheer/gunwale 1   Forefoot 6   Skeg 11
Flared section 2   Ballast Keel 7   Transom 12
Stem 3   Keel 8   Tumblehome section 13
Waterline 4   Run 9   Buttock line 14
Entry 5   Deadrise 10

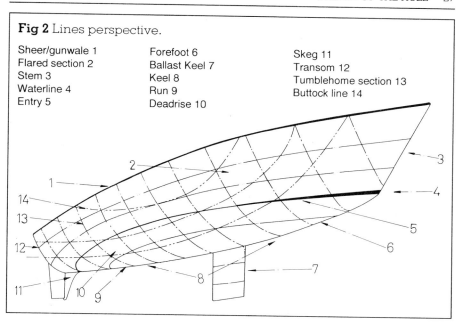

tended to become unbalanced as the angle of heel increased, since the bow would be inclined to lift whilst the lack of buoyancy in the aft sections immersed the stern more deeply. Not surprisingly, an uncomfortable pitching moment was the inevitable accompaniment to a hard slog to windward.

This 'cod's head and mackerel tail' type of hull form was largely superseded, particularly in lighter boats, by a long and fine entry coupled to a broad high-volume stern which often made it possible to plane or surf, albeit rather erratically. In spite of the unsettling habit of running out of rudder, if hard-pressed as the bow immerses and the buoyant stern lifts, this design has several very positive attributes. First of all, the Vee'd sections forward slice through waves rather than being deflected by them (although the crew will be treated to a wet ride in anything of a chop) and secondly, it makes sound logistical sense. After all, on any small boat space is very much at a premium: gas and fuel, possibly an outboard, to say nothing of three or four crew members, will all be jammed right aft in the cockpit, so that beamy stern is quite a load-carrying asset! Waterline beam on this type tends to be rather narrow and, consequently, the boats only turn in an optimum performance if sailed upright. Unfortunately, though, the lack of form stability ensures that the crew will either have to reef early or at least keep their weight up to weather.

Windage and aesthetics

The light displacement boat of the 90's tends towards a better balanced waterline, though still rather narrow. The U-shaped bow sections provides lift in a seaway, the run aft has buoyant sections so is unlikely to dig in too deeply, and throughout the middle range of wind and wave strengths performance and tractability are at a maximum. But the boat is still at its best sailed with minimal angle of heel; at angles beyond about 20° the drag of the heeled topsides will slow the vessel drastically.

Whatever the waterline shape the hull speed is dependent upon its length, and it is partly for this reason that long overhangs at bow and stern were always favoured for displacement racing boats; once heeled, the overhang effectively elongated the waterline. The overhanging bow and counter can also, to some extent, dampen a pitching moment. They are, however, expensive in terms of wasted space, to say nothing of mooring charges based on the overall length and, where a timber boat is concerned, also very prone to rot and distortion.

The sections of the lines drawing, when read as a single entity, show the wetted surface, displacement and form stability, but the midships sections also demonstrate the available accommodation space. Leaving this last to one side for the moment and thinking about the performance of the hull, it can be seen that, for a particular displacement, a semi-circular form offers the lowest drag because of the small waterline beam; it is, though, the least initially stable and may require a disproportionate amount of ballast to enable the hull to stand up to its sail area: ergo, increased cost of keel or internal ballast. There is, too, a tendency for a hull of this shape to roll murderously downwind (also when at anchor) a propensity exacerbated by the high topsides and shallow draft which often go together with the type.

A hull with a sharper – that is to say, squarer – turn down to the bilge will have greater stability initially but there will be less immersed volume below the water. So except on boats where headroom is regarded as an unnecessary concession to decadence, any slight gain in stability will be paid for by the increase in freeboard – automatically carrying with it an increase in windage and heeling moment!

The topsides (the upper part of the hull) not only focus the eye upon the shape and visual appeal of the boat, but play a decisive role in the seaworthiness and room below decks – and these are more closely interrelated than might be supposed at first sight. Windage is proportionately greater in a small boat than a larger one – often to the point where an excess may prevent the boat making any headway at all to windward in a blow. Think of a 20-foot cruising boat slogging it out in a force 6. It will be well reefed down, probably with the sail area reduced to 100 square feet or thereabouts. The topside and coachroof area presented to the wind will be about half that of the sails – but unlike the sails, none of that windage will be convertible into forward motion.

However, the height of the topsides does affect the dryness of the boat in a seaway. Usually there will be a slight flare – an outward curve where the greatest breadth is at deck level. This, in theory, flings spray clear of the bows rather into the cockpit and down the necks of the crew. The additional buoyancy is also claimed to minimise pitching as the shape softens the effect of pounding into – or rather on to – waves. A knuckle moulded into the topsides forwards is claimed to be even more efficacious. It undoubtedly has some effect – and increases the space in the forecabin – but does little to improve either appearance or the heeled shape of the hull.

The opposite to flare is known as tumblehome: here the topsides curve in towards the gunwale, in section rather similar to a brandy snifter. This means that the beam at deck level may be six inches less than at the midpoint between it and the waterline and, in consequence, there will be a little weight saved on deck. There should be a slight reduction in drag too as the clutter of tracks, stanchions and guardwires adorning the deck edge are kept clear of the water!

Nowadays, on smaller sailing craft, it is usual for the sheerline to be uncompromisingly flat, that gentle concave swoop from bow to stern deemed passé. In truth, the conventional sheer would look out of place on a pared down GRP production boat with high freeboard and short ends. But the 'classic' sheerline did not evolve simply to enhance the appearance of the handsome yachts and working boats of the first half of this century; it served to keep the craft dry and, in addition, to provide a reserve of buoyancy and stability which could actually prevent a fatal knock-down. But it does create turbulence when the boat heels and is not too helpful so far as the accommodation is concerned either, since it makes for good headroom in the forepeak while taking it from the midships living area! Hogged or reverse sheer is more practical, where bows and stern are lower than the midships and, as a consequence somewhat lighter. With extra height midships, the coachroof height can be cut down without adversely affecting headroom. Like tumblehome, in its most extreme form it is downright ugly – but then, so are most designers' excesses!

Naturally, the process of designing a yacht is more complicated than this outline might suggest. There are few boats where some compromise does not have to be made – and in the case of a boat intended for production building, these may be numerous. The conflicting demands of accommodation, light weight and shoal draft demanded of a trailer sailer call for a skilled juggling with dimensions and specifications of the construction if the finished product is to be rugged enough to withstand offshore sailing, look acceptable, and handle sweetly – yet remain competitively priced in a keenly contested market place. And now, one of the demands of that market place is that not only shall the yacht be self-righting, but it shall also be unsinkable, with sufficient in-built buoyancy to support the swamped hull. Back, as they say, to the drawing board.

3 The Accommodation

No matter how well the designer fulfils the brief to produce an attractive, wholesome and handy trailer sailer, it is in many cases the layout, the (sometimes misleading) air of spaciousness and the sheer ingenuity of the accommodation which will be the main selling point. This does not necessarily delight the designers even if the majority are grimly resigned to it, although I personally know one who habitually drew the interior to a different, more optimistic scale and then simply left it to the builder to sort matters out! While this is not the norm, I would strongly advise anyone to use a tape measure on some of the 'full length' and 'double' berths tucked under sidedecks and odd corners of small yachts!

What is required from the layout does depend a great deal on the type of sailing envisage; clearly, passage-making for several days and nights at sea imposes different demands from daysailing or occasional week-ending, where pubs, restaurants and other shoreside conveniences are handy. With a trailer sailer, too, the feasibility of living on board with any semblance of comfort while the yacht is on the trailer en route to the sailing venue needs to be borne in mind. So, by its very nature, the boat must combine domestic qualities equally at home on land or sea. These can seem mutually incompatible since layouts which are perfectly functional when upright, in harbour or on the trailer, become untenable when thrashing along in a wind over tide chop, heeled to 40° and plummeting gaily into every hole in the sea! The gadgets of everyday life develop a hostile animation all their own: sinks cease to drain, securely fixed cookers jettison saucepans of scalding soup, loose gear hurls itself around the cabin with the malevolence of a poltergeist and the loo, discretely tucked away under the forward berth cushions becomes, to put it delicately, impractical to use!

Taking a 20-footer as an example (about the average size for a trailer sailer), at least seven feet of the overall length, and in the widest part at that, will be taken up by the cockpit. At the bow, between two and three feet will be usable only for the stowage of anchor and cable. Given a maximum beam of eight feet, this leaves an area of around 100 sq ft

which can be used for accommodation. If this space was rec
tangular, it would be a simple matter to fit in four berths,
table, galley and lavatory along with adequate stowage for
crockery, personal effects, water and ship's stores.
Unfortunately, it is not: it is wedge shaped. It is the art o
putting this awkward space to the best possible use which
distinguishes a designer who has lived aboard a small yach
from one who dismisses the human frame as a structure
which requires a volume of six feet by two feet by eighteen
inches and which can simply be stacked away like firewood
when not needed to work the vessel!

Manufacturers' brochures will state that their boat is able
to sleep four adults in comfort; occasionally, in flights of fancy
they claim berths for five or six. While it is not impossible, for
even four adults to co-exist for any length of time on board a
boat in this size range suggests a degree of amiable compan-
ionship which is rare, even within a close-knit family. Once
under way, those adults will be navigating, washing,
attempting to cook and eat meals and generally carry on
some semblance of normal life. In bad weather, everyone
wants to get below out of the wind, in fine weather they all
want to relax in the cockpit and overcrowd that! The French,
however, do adapt to – and even apparently enjoy – cruising
with a complement that justifies the wildest claims as to a
small yacht's carrying capacity: in harbour, not only will the
cockpit be filled to bursting point by the crew, their friends,
offspring and small dogs, but it will also overflow with the
trappings of the good life: cushions, ice boxes, parasols, bar-
becues and food and drink in unbelievable quantities!

An element of privacy

Having a high regard for privacy, the British tend to favour a
two-cabin layout on all but the very smallest craft. This certainly suits those with young children whose most active and
noisy hours seem rarely to correspond with those of their par-
ents. The motion of the boat is more noticeable forward but
this rarely worries youngsters, although the noise of a boat
sailing hard can occasionally prove unsettling. Of course, the
lavatory in small boats is usually sited between the forward
berths and, with the forecabin occupied, this can be seen as a
bit of a drawback.

Separate after cabins are not unknown on trailer sailers;

this arrangement certainly gives privacy although it is obtained at the cost of a reduction in cockpit area – arguably no great disadvantage for an offshore cruising boat – or by a reduction of space in the main cabin. However, unless the aft cabin is of sufficient size to boast its own 'en suite' facilities, there may well be times when the occupants have an urgent need to disturb those trying to get their heads down in the fore part of the boat!

There are one or two yachts, slightly over 20 feet in length – and very beamy in proportion to that length – where a miniature aft cabin (or in fact usually a large quarter berth with dividing door) runs aft, under cockpit seat and sidedeck. Although offering little more room than the cell of an anchorite, these 'semi-cabins' do offer total seclusion and so are excellent for a couple of youngsters (or one and a half seriously exhausted adults). Ventilation, though, will be poor if the scuttle to the cockpit has to be shut and, should an inboard engine be fitted to the boat, its sturdy thumping in use will be very close to the ears of the occupants.

With all berths in a single cabin, the through-flow of air will at least be good. The importance of adequate ventilation should not be overlooked, but is often disregarded except when the cook is concocting a chicken Madras or when weather conditions are such that the main hatch has to be kept closed, though if any direct form of cabin heating is employed, ventilation becomes absolutely vital. It is true, of course, that with an open plan layout a degree of intimacy must be tolerated, and there will inevitably be times when the machinations of navigator or cook disturb those who are attempting to snatch some sleep and this, when passage-making, may lead to ill-temper or worse, sheer exhaustion after a couple of days.

As a selling point, all single berths are usually claimed to be full length, the implication being that they are six feet six inches long. Often only a couple actually will be, the remainder being a few inches shorter. This is worth checking although in all honesty, unless especially selected for brawn (as a racing crew might be) a crew with all members over six feet tall would be a rarity. That said, a tall person of robust build would be uncomfortably restricted by the average quarter berth (partially under the cockpit sidebenches) or by a bunk in a 'trotter box', where a section of it runs in a trunking under galley fitments or perhaps into the forecabin.

A restless adult might also find a pilot berth (which is really little more than a glorified shelf behind a settee) little to his or her taste, although to those who can withstand the occasional close encounter with deckhead or chainplate braces, this berth becomes a remarkably snug and desirable pit once at sea. This serves to underline the fact that comfort at sea is not necessarily the same as – or compatible with – comfort in harbour or marina. Double berths are notorious in this respect: for a start, the dimensions are almost always less than those of a shoreside version and so a couple may find themselves cramped, even when the boat is on an even keel. When the yacht begins sailing on its ear, the occupants will find themselves wedged together on the lee side, unless the berth cushions are separated along the centreline by a lee-cloth. Lee-cloths are essential on all seagoing berths – safer than boards which can bruise the sleeper or possibly injure anyone flung against them when the going gets rough.

Few would pretend that sleeping on board a small boat is always an altogether delightful experience. Even when the berths are adequately-sized, the foam cushions, under

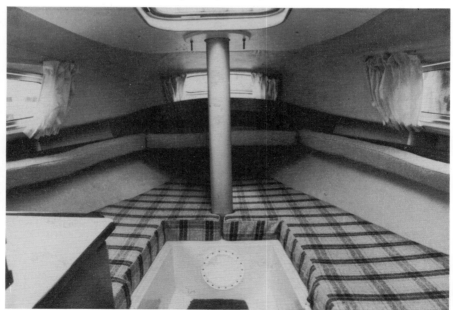

The neat forecabin of a junk rigged Coromandel showing the keel stepped mast. This is hinged just above the coachroof for easier raising and lowering.

compression by the human anatomy, lose all resilience and it is almost guaranteed that the occupant, if he sleeps at all, will wake up stiff and tired. Deeper foam helps up to a point, but beyond six inches (the average cushion is three, sometimes four inches thick) the mattress will tend to become hot and clammy. Also, the increased thickness will restrict headroom slightly. The secret is to substitute webbing for the unyielding wood of the berth soles though this is not always possible in the case of a glassfibre boat where the berths are part of an internal moulding. The webbing allows ventilation, so minimising condensation and, although canvas webbing will need tightening at the end of each season, the contribution to comfort is remarkable. But beware of rubber webbing: with the yacht under way, the elasticity will make the berth as springy as a trampoline!

The galley

The galley space is the part of the accommodation most likely to be curtailed by the keel or plate box, though in a beamy lift-keeler, the intrusion will be minimal as the casing can nearly always be incorporated into joinery and worktop. In a narrow-gutted yacht, to fit in a cooker, sink, stowage for both stores and crockery and to provide sufficient usable working surfaces involves a good deal of juggling. Also it is, all too often, a self-defeating exercise. At sea, nothing succeeds like simplicity. Forget those tricky little sliding chopping boards and hinge-down worktops which are too small to set a saucepan down on – none of these are worth a damn in a small cruising boat: they may even be hazardous. Sinks, too, are a waste of time unless they really are deep enough to cope with a full load of washing-up and are fitted with a separate discharge pump: two large buckets are far more use!

The siting of the galley has been a matter of controversy since the evolution of the yacht and the decline of the coal-burning bogey stove. When it was common practice for even a small yacht to ship a paid hand, or at least a lad to help out with domestic chores, both crew member and galley were unceremoniously housed in the forepeak and left to their own devices. This siting has little to recommend it: not only is space cramped and headroom minimal, but the boat's motion is always at its most lively forward. Also, ventilation will be virtually non-existent since opening the forehatch under way is guaranteed to extinguish both the stove and the cook's enthusiasm for the task in hand.

If the galley is to be fitted in around the keel box it will probably be situated amidships, possibly with cooker to one side, worktop to the other and a demountable table top between. On a larger craft, there is often space to construct the galley adjacent to the companionway and to use part of the step as a working area, though this layout means doing away with the quarter berth. However, siting it here is quite advantageous so far as ventilation, relative ease of motion and headroom are concerned – and proximity to the cockpit when the helmsman fancies a quick cuppa.

Accepting that all things domestic on a small yacht involve a high degree of give and take, there is an understandable temptation to sacrifice a really practical galley in order to get in an extra berth, even when this entails putting the stove under (or occasionally over) a bunk, in a locker which hinges down from the shipside, or interring it beneath the bridgedeck, where it can slide it out on runners for use. None of these arrangements is satisfactory whether from the point of efficiency, cleanliness or safety. Indeed the last siting in particular is one which should be condemned absolutely. The difficulty of escaping in the event of fire (and many fires do break out in the galley) is all too real and must never be overlooked. But all boats are fitted with a forehatch which can be used as an emergency escape route, aren't they? Astonishing though it may seem, the answer is – no, they are not and this is to be deplored. Quite a number of small cruising yachts, whether of timber or GRP construction, have entirely dispensed with this item on the grounds that (a) it may leak (b) it may weaken the deck and (c) it is unnecessarily expensive! Though fitting a hatch to an existing wooden boat may not be beyond the ability of the average owner, doing the same with a glassfibre yacht calls for the services of a skilled professional and, depending on the design of the deck and coachroof, is likely to prove both difficult and costly.

The type of cooker, or more accurately, its fuel, is largely up to personal preference. Such preferences are often fiercely held, unchangeable and, dare it be said, not strictly based on logic – or at least on experience. Liquid petroleum gas (LPG) seems to have received a bad press; unquestionably, some concern is expressed as to its safety. The possible risk attendant upon its use is well known: since gas is heavier than air, if a leak develops in the system (or a burner is unwittingly left turned on) it sinks to the bilges, awaiting only one spark to cause an explosion. This being the case, it goes without saying that correct installation, maintenance and monitoring of all pipework, appliances and connections are of paramount importance. Just the same, accidents do occur from time to time, as of course they do in the home. Often though, accidents are directly attributable to carelessness and, no matter how carefully safety standards are laid down and enforced, it is impossible to legislate against human error.

Both pressurised paraffin and alcohol have their devotees and their detractors. Personally I dislike the priming which is an essential preliminary to lighting a pressure paraffin stove, and I must also confess to being less than enthusiastic about the low heat, invisible flame and occasional fumes associated with alcohol, as well as the difficulty of buying the correct alcohol in Britain; meths is a barely acceptable substitute – though if mixed with 10% water, combustion is cleaner and almost odourless. Personal prejudices are, as I said, hard to alter.

Over the years, it has been my ill-fortune to be forced into preparing food on an assortment of jury-rigged contrivances, including an old sock, saturated in meths and stuck in a corned beef tin! Looking back, I turn pale at the thought of such risks and hardly dare to contemplate the reaction of any marine insurance underwriter who may be reading this. However, there is no-one so self-righteous as a poacher turned gamekeeper and now, naturally, I cook in a conventional manner over an approved stove. If you are tempted to 'make do', bear in mind that there exists a proliferation of formal rules and specifications, all of which must be complied with: failure to do so will invalidate the boat's insurance. No matter whether gas, alcohol or paraffin is employed for cooking, the appliance, fuel containers and lines must conform to the relevant standards.

Civilised dining

The type of fuel is not, of course, the only point of contention so far as the cooker is concerned: argument is rife as to its optimum size. There are crews who subsist largely upon warmed-up concoctions ladled from tin or packet, and for their gastronomic forays a single burner will be quite adequate. Others go to the opposite extreme, demanding three courses with all the trimmings three times a day; for these nothing less than a multi-burner cooker with oven and grill will do, even though such a sophisticated *batterie de cuisine* will gulp fuel at an alarming rate. While a grill is invaluable – if only for the production of toasted sandwiches or the re-heating of leftovers – an oven is a doubtful asset. Quite apart from its appetite for fuel, it adds a good deal of weight and, on a small yacht, there may not be room for the cooker to swing freely when gimballed – and gimballed it must be if it is to be used under way. Ambitious cooking is bound to require plenty of worktop space and involve more than one pan or casserole thereby generating masses of washing up! So, on balance, unless the boat is custom-designed around the galley space – and few trailer sailers are – keep it simple; stick to a two-burner appliance with a grill. If there is an adventurous ship's cook on board, one who delights in baking bread or cakes, it is possible to buy collapsible stove-top ovens – also a variety of dry-cook pans, griddles and other such aids. Since any cooker must be fitted with fiddle rails, the selection of pans is worth a thought – none must be so shallow as to slide or jam its handles underneath the rails.

As with working areas, secure stowage space for breakable items is always at a premium – proceed on the basis that if a dish can smash it will – and if it does it will be the one most valued. Where purpose-moulded stowage for cups, plates, etc is not part of the overall design, adjustable pegs will keep contents in place as will drop-down partitions in larger lockers. Once again, simplicity is the keynote: open cave lockers allow inspection of the contents at a glance. They also allow air circulation, don't add unnecessary weight and have no doors to rattle or fling themselves open at the least convenient moment. Drawers, which on a small boat can only be fitted lengthwise in a unit, are also a nuisance since they either fly out when the boat heels or else defy all efforts to prise them open.

Not that all the angst is confined to the preparation of a meal: the business of actually eating it can also be rather fraught, especially when the weather is boisterous. In such conditions any pretence of formal table manners must be abandoned and, if the crew are able to slurp a mug of soup or gnaw hastily at a sandwich, they can probably count themselves fortunate. Given the unpredictable, often violent, motion and minimal internal volume of a small cruiser, there is always an element of 'roughing it' which simply has to be shrugged off – but it is nevertheless pleasant to retain a

Fig 3

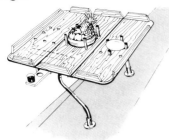

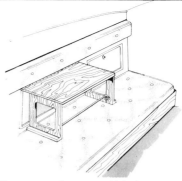

a If there is room for it, this type of drop flap table approaches the ideal, being sturdy and well fiddled with the fiddles removable so the table can be easily swept clear of crumbs and debris. The drop flaps, supported by lopers when raised, can bang around when lowered so secure them with a cabin hook or bolt. Tapered pegs slotting into holes keep dishes in place, and there is a pull out slide which will take drinks tumblers – or even bottles. But even though the supports are angled so as to keep the passage through the cabin as clear as possible, only a beamy boat would find space for such an extensive piece of woodwork – and no racing fanatic would be too keen on the weight of it either!

b Where space is very restricted small tray/tables which hinge down from backrests or cave lockers are handy – best to put a protective covering on the berth underneath before eating though!

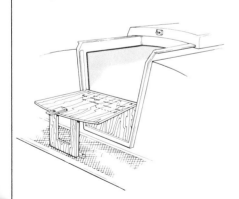

c A simple demountable table which can be set up in a moment on a washboard – a hinged support simply inserts into a permanent tongue on the lower washboard.

d A saloon table on a column which can be raised to the deckhead so as to occupy less room when not in use.

semblance of civilisation in fine weather or when safely berthed in harbour (or cruising overland). To dine in comfort, if not splendour, calls for some basic essentials – the first being a table, rigid and possessed of sufficient area for the diners' plates, cruet, cutlery and elbows. The need for adequate seating room is obvious, but less so is the necessity for leg room which is not always allowed for.

The trouble with a centreline saloon table is simply that it occupies a disproportionate amount of space and, unless it also can be used for chartwork, this is space wasted for most of the time. However, it may prove impracticable to fit any other type, given a centreplate or keel box and at least in this 'conventional' arrangement, with settee berths either side, there will be leg and elbow room. The problem is where to hide the table when it is not actively in use: of course if it forms part of a dinette this problem can be discounted as it will be offset and out of the way and, at night, it will generally be converted to a double berth. Otherwise it is just a nuisance, barring the passage forward and generally getting in the way. Drop flaps fitted to a centreline table help, but only marginally if the cabin sole is narrow. An increasingly common practice – and one which works well – is for the table to be constructed around a pillar which may also serve as the mast compression strut (and form a useful grabrail too). The table is secured by a screw collar which not only means that height can be adjusted for dining but makes it possible to slide the table right up against the deckhead when it is not needed. Tables mounted on single or twin pillars screwed into the sole can be demounted and the component parts stashed away in lockers when they would otherwise be in the way but, although the operation only takes a few minutes, the temptation is not to bother and leave it in situ.

All tables need to be fitted with fiddle rails and it is best if these are simply dowelled into place so that they can easily be removed for cleaning the top. A solid table which is left permanently in place may find room for fitted bottle racks; these are expensive to construct but very welcome in certain circumstances. To avoid injury to the crew, all tables, indeed all internal furnishings, should have rounded corners, and whether the table top is raised, lowered or juggled around with, it does help if catches and screw fitments work properly. Revolving – or worse – descending dining tables may be the stuff of slapstick comedy but a hungry crew or harassed cook may not see the joke.

The other domestic utility

And now, to deal with the last of the domestic fixtures, the lavatory. In view of the embarrassment accompanying any discussion of this installation it is rather ironic that often it is this item of a yacht's inventory that is the single most important selling point; disappointing in view of the avowed constant search for improved sailing qualities, speed and all-round dependability, but there it is.

But, logically, why should there be any eyebrows raised at what is, after all a perfectly valid expectation? Surely it is not too much to ask of any boat intended for family cruising that it be duly furnished with a lavatory, and sufficient room to make use of it, in private and without undue contortion. Neither is it unreasonable to expect good ventilation and adjacent surfaces which are easily cleaned. Well, unfortunately, few yachts under 24 feet in length overall do measure up to these expectations, although there are one or two which have tried hard even when they have paid dearly in terms of galley space and stowage. But, to my way of thinking, a chemical or flushing toilet wedged beneath a berth, as it all too often has to be, is just about useless given normal human consideration for others who may be sharing the accommodation. Even so, quite a few people are prepared to put up with the illusion of privacy created by a curtained forepeak and are, presumably, equally prepared to turn out the occupants of the forward berths when it is deemed necessary.

The traditional time-honoured flushing marine WC – as typified by the Baby Blake – often instigated a love/hate relationship. In fairness to a fine piece of sanitary engineering, a certain amount of disharmony could be attributed to carelessness – all marine toilets do need to be treated with respect as regards both maintenance and use. Flushing toilets can easily become clogged, although normally this only happens through unfamiliarity with the operating instructions, or disregard of them. Manually operated models need vigorous pumping – and the indelicate sound of this operation may itself bring a flush to sensitive cheeks. So far as a trailer sailer is concerned, marine lavatories have the undeniable drawback that they cannot be used when overland cruising. Obviously they should, in any case, only be used in tidal waters and are banned from discharging into inland waterways and some rivers. In an increasing number of areas regulations require that a holding tank must be fitted.

Another argument against fitting a flushing WC is that holes have to be drilled in the yacht's underbody so that you then have to rely upon hoses, clips and seacocks to maintain watertight integrity. For this reason alone, many people avoid installing one and either opt for the mark one bucket or a chemical toilet. These are lightweight, well designed and odour-free in normal use even if, initially, the experience of waiting with receptacle in line at a pump-out station may be mildly embarrassing! The smaller versions are remarkably low priced and it is not a bad idea, if cruising with a full crew, to have a second 'facility' stowed (securely) in a cockpit locker where it can be used when the boat is either on the trailer or moored with a cockpit tent in place.

Cleaning up

A modern glassfibre boat, with internal surfaces finished in gel or melamine laminate is easy to keep clean, not so a wooden boat whose angles and corners of joinery form traps for damp and dirt and whose woodwork calls for constant attention with paint and varnish brush. But at least painted surfaces can be re-touched; scorch marks or chips on GRP are not easy to disguise and melamine laminate is very unsightly once scuffed or scored. Domestic chores take up a fair bit of time in even the smallest boat – and the more complex the interior fixtures and fittings, the more time will be spent scrubbing and polishing! There are of course those who will happily admit that they suffer from the so-called 'Diogenes syndrome' and wish for nothing more than to enjoy simplicity which, to be honest, is often no more than a synonym for squalor. Not that there is anything wrong with this, indeed a degree of muddle is inseparable from existence on board, especially with a full complement. But there are few things more depressing, especially in bad weather when everyone may be confined below, than to see nothing but dirty dishes, and a frowsty cabin; it can sap the will to keep going. Prosaic as it sounds, this is reason enough to spend that little thought – even money – on the accommodation. It makes for a happier crew and that nearly always means a safer one.

4 Multihulls

More than a generation has passed since the appearance on the European scene of the cruising multihull but the species is, even today, looked upon with misgiving. Those who choose to sail catamarans – or even more outrageous – trimarans, are regarded as eccentric by those who prefer to voyage to their destination in a 'proper' yacht: that is a mono-hull with a nice deep ballast keel. Admittedly, to judge by the chequered careers of some of the enormous offshore racing multihulls, those extrovert, often experimental, sailing machines, there seems some truth in the idea that the multi-hull is, by nature, a dangerous means of transport and to venture forth in one is to take a calculated risk. But, of course, these skeletal structures, stressed to the limit, with weight pared to the very bone, are designed first to win races and second to attract publicity for their sponsors. But these machines have little to do with the real world of the cruising cat or tri. These craft, whose sizes range from about 20 feet to upwards of 60, many of them amateur-built, travel between them millions of miles each year under sail, without incident, trauma or loss of life. True, they do have their bad points as well as good and are not perhaps ideally suited for a begin-ner to helm because the reactions tend to be snappy.

Those opposed to the very idea of a multihull as a cruiser reiterate the drawbacks which are inevitably, if erroneously, associated with the designs in general: lack of manoeuvrabil-ity, poor windward performance, a propensity for capsizing without warning and inherent structural weakness leading to leakage, or worse, a complete break-up. Add to this the claim that accommodation is poor when taking into account the overall length and it is not difficult to see why there is preju-dice against these craft.

The 'anti' lobby could be accused of overstating its case, and indeed it certainly would be by all multihull aficionados.

Different species

Before attempting to counter these arguments, it must be

remembered that, for a start, catamarans and trimarans are very dissimilar beasts, not only from monohulls, but also from each other. The design of each individual cat or tri will also differ according to the designer's mandate. Basically, however, both types can be sub-divided (as can monohulls to some degree) into light and fast or sedate and sumptuous, though many do claim to combine the best of both worlds.

To those attracted to multihulls, the sheer speed is exhilarating even if others may find it nothing short of intimidating! Although there are singular examples which serve as the contradictions proving any rule, for a given hull length even a relatively heavy cruising multihull will return higher speeds than its single-hulled counterpart: speeds usually measured in double figures and occasionally recorded in the region of 20 knots. Such startling performance is nearly always achieved when reaching in a flat sea with a moderate to strong breeze. (Because of the high hull speed, the apparent wind is brought forward of the beam so that the sheets of most multihulls are only freed away in light airs.) Acceleration, even in a dedicated cruising boat, is rapid – astonishing to those more at home with 'conventional' craft: deceleration is frequently just as abrupt. Either mode can alarm the unwary!

The oft-derided cussedness of a multihull when it comes to tacking or, for that matter, deviating in any way from the straight and narrow, is not entirely a myth. A catamaran, having in many cases almost twice as much wetted surface (and keel length) as a trimaran of comparable length (which will only rarely have all three hulls immersed at any given moment) will be, on the whole, the less co-operative type when it comes to slaloming through a congested waterway. Tacking a cat is always easier if the boat is not allowed to lose headway; it may be necessary to bear away fractionally so as to increase speed before coming through the eye of the wind or, if the beast is really bloody-minded about it, apply coercion in the form of a backed headsail. Reluctance to bear away is often directly attributable to a helmsman attempting the manoeuvre with the mainsheet still pinned in hard – even a monohull will resent such treatment and refuse to oblige.

Windward performance, as in the case of any sailing vessel, depends to a great extent upon windage of topsides, superstructure and rig and the vertical depth of the underbody. So, in the interest of efficiency, some multihulls, in particular many of the smaller, livelier boats, increase lateral resistance with pivoting or lifting unballasted boards of timber or glassfibre. These do slightly increase production costs and decrease accommodation space (though that space, so far as any trailable multihull is concerned, is going to be pretty minimal anyway). Generally in a catamaran there is one plate or board in each hull; with a trimaran, a single board is more likely to be fitted, within the main central hull. Cruising multis in the main have a low aspect mini keel, unballasted (although several designs do fit water tanks within part of the structure) and short enough to have little adverse effect on manoeuvrability. Others rely upon the shape and section (often assymetric) of the immersed hull, as do many of the deeply Vee'd derivatives of the Polynesian cats designed by James Wharram.

The capsize risk

Any multihull sailor will always be aware of the possibility of complete inversion, although perhaps not to the extent that the uninitiated might suppose. Even the most stolid of cats might fly a hull if brutally mishandled, but no multihull, unless caught by a rogue wave, is likely to capsize without prior warning. The experienced helmsman might sense the danger point, but for the newcomer the warning is mainly visual: when the wake of the weather hull fines away and the lee hull throws up a heavy rooster tail of spray, it is time to slow down, reef and contemplate strategy. At night, where the 'handle with care' signs cannot be seen, restraint is strongly advised; far better to set too little sail area than too much.

In theory, the rig of many multihulls is designed to give way before the vessel will overturn. It is, of course, better not to put this to the test as calculations are not invariably correct. Various devices have been conceived to back up the helmsman's judgement – or misjudgement! Masthead floats, air bags, operated on impact with the water, and electrical sensors which let fly the mainsheet at a pre-determined loading have all been tried with varying degrees of success. For the worst case scenario, experiments have been carried out with an ingenious system of ballast tanks which bring bows or stern clear of the water and de-stabilise the capsized craft to the extent that it can easily be righted.

But, the voice of reason asserts, if multihulls capsize, so do monohulls. Well, yes, they do from time to time although it is pretty rare; knock-downs, though, with the masthead touching the water are not so uncommon and, if a hatch is open at the time, the boat may well be swamped. But complete 360° rolls do take place and with results which can be imagined. Ballasted yachts have inverted completely and the crew have lived to tell the tale: after such a case, dismasting is almost universal, injury to crew members usual and widespread damage to hull and superstructure inevitable. How many yachts founder after such an incident will never really be known: the reason for this gap in statistics is, regrettably, all too obvious. A capsized multihull will, on the other hand, normally remain afloat, occasionally for days or even weeks but in nearly all cases for a sufficient length of time to allow the crew to take to the liferaft.

Rather less well documented is a capsize stern over bows, otherwise known as pitchpoling. This is mainly generated – or at least exacerbated – by wave action and occurs as a result of the multihull's fine bows burying themselves as the stern lifts to a steep following sea: the point of no return is reached and a somersault follows, often with attendant damage to the capsized hull. Prudence and avoidance of such conditions is the only safeguard but no cruising yacht of whatever size or type can possibly guarantee this. As with other disasters, pitchpoling is not restricted to multihulls, although in severe weather a multihull's only safe answer may be to run for it, there may be a greater statistical risk.

Broaching, where the stern whips around in a following sea and the boat is briefly brought beam on, is very dangerous to any class of vessel. It is, though, arguably more dangerous to a ballasted monohull than to a cat or tri. Injury to rig and rudder, possibly even to the crew, may result but a multi, due to its greater buoyancy, will probably escape without being totally swamped. So long as the rudders are of adequate depth, a multi may be less inclined to broach wildly in the first place, since the twin (or triple) hulls have excellent directional stability. If the ultimate storm ever materialises, pitchpoling is almost certainly the greater risk.

Can multihulls self-destruct?

Basic structural weakness, whether due to a shortcoming in the design or the construction, is often cited as reasonable grounds for steering clear of the multihull. There is a germ of truth in this view. Not only racing but also cruising multis have indeed been reported as breaking up and, on occasion, doing so without apparent reason. In reality, the likelihood of instant self-destruction is greatly exaggerated and owes more to propaganda than proven fact. In almost all cases, those which have disintegrated have been death-or-glory racing boats, hell-bent on trophies and records. Others have been built by amateurs who misguidedly buy a set of plans which promise that timber and glassfibre can, at very little cost, be transformed into a seaworthy boat in which they can sail off into the tropical sunset. Unfortunately, some do just exactly that. Such cunning salesmanship is targeted towards those whose boundless but uninformed enthusiasm is not necessarily backed up either by hard cash or woodworking skills and it has certainly helped to give some types of multihull a bad name.

Some, of course, do disintegrate after grounding or collision but errors in navigation, pilotage or seamanship can hardly be blamed upon the boat itself. Perhaps it is fair to say that a lightweight cat or tri might just suffer severe damage from an incident that a substantial monohull could survive, if not unscathed, at least intact. Even this, though, is open to argument: circumstances alter cases. A 'conventional' yacht of traditional construction, even when built like the proverbial brick outhouse, may spring planks, break ribs or, in the case of a glassfibre boat, loosen bulkheads and internal fittings. If holed, almost any ballasted boat may fall victim to the negative buoyancy factor – or, to put it another way, be dragged down by the weight of its keel!

On balance, the modern multihull has a lot going for it, and the technology of today has made possible not only a reduction in weight but a simplification of cross-beam and bridgedeck members, thus speeding up the process of dismantling (and re-assembly) for trailing.

With the possible exception of the 26-foot Telstar trimaran, and some custom built one-off designs, small trailable multis do lose out on accommodation space below decks and, once the craft is folded for trailing, life aboard is going to be reduced to the bare necessities. And there are very few production boats of sufficient length to be seriously considered for cruising, as opposed to daysailing, which can be trailed without at least partial demolition; indeed the 20-foot Cracksman, whose beam is only 8 feet can probably claim to

Strider – an attractive and nimble 24 foot demountable catamaran with spartan accommodation.

be the only one. This gives it a real edge when cruising over-land since the crew can probably make good use of the deck and cockpit space.

Practical pros and cons

Having stated that the majority of trailer sailing cats and tris are fairly simple to ready for launching, it still takes a fair bit of time. The 24-foot Strider, a sporty and attractive lightweight cat, with berths for two in each of the twin hulls, can be read-ied in 45 minutes from start to finish, but, in all honesty, only by a crew well accustomed to the process. But there is never-theless no great difficulty in the operation and the sprightly performance and crisp handling of the cat amply repay the effort.

Similar in concept are the Wharram-designed 23-foot Hina and 21 and 26-foot Tiki designs. All provide simple accommodation within each hull, acres of deck and cockpit room for their size and, depending upon the rig selected, turn in very creditable performances. Although more at home sailing in coastal waters, perhaps with an occasional cross-Channel dash in settled weather, one Tiki 26, albeit with very experienced crew, has made an Atlantic crossing.

All these small cats have similar drawbacks – they are extremely wet to sail and the cockpit is totally exposed with nowhere at all for the crew to shelter away from wind and waves. Fine, enjoyable even, during the summer months, but out of season the crew really would need to wear wetsuits. Also, leaving aside the question of living space (which more closely resembles some sort of filing system for human beings), room for stowage, especially of weighty items such as fuel for the outboard, water, tinned supplies etc is also scarce; a Strider, for example, can be fitted with berths for four as well as a rudimentary galley and simple chemical toilet but four adults would be hard put to carry enough supplies to see them through more than a couple of days.

Small trimarans, such as the 25-foot Typhoon, an ultra-light and exceptionally rapid item of sailing hardware which makes use of a pair of Tornado cat hulls as the outriggers, can hardly be described as dry when under way but the cockpit is partly protected by the main accommodation bulkhead and this does keep off a bit of the green stuff. In many cases, too, it is quite feasible to increase the shelter by fitting a folding spray cover over the main hatchway and this does bring about a remarkable improvement. The accommodation of a trimaran, depending of course upon the size and type, does more closely approach what the average human would regard as the norm: enough headroom to sit in comfort, enough floor to give an illusion of leg room beneath the dining table (precious few small cats can boast a civilised dining table) and just that little extra space for galley and lavatory. But the difficulty of stowing heavy stores is still there, since the outriggers of a small tri can carry only the lightest of loads – sails and oilskins, for example.

The 26-foot Dragonfly is rather less Spartan and achieves a good compromise between speed and interior space. The hulls fold inboard at the tug of a line and this minimises

The Typhoon trimaran – not for the faint hearted as it accelerates to speeds of around fourteen knots as though a fuse has been lit. The light tri, easy to trail once dismantled, uses Tornado class catamaran hulls as outriggers. Accommodation is nothing to shout about, but two tough adults would find it acceptable – the performance really outweighs all other considerations!

marina charges. Such engineering and design sophistication is, however, quite expensive!

So, at the end of the day, the small multihull can be seen as a viable proposition for trailer sailing; not everyone's choice for sure and not without negative qualities either. It is best suited to those who put speed first and relegate any thoughts of home comforts in the conventional sense further down the list.

But plus-points like speed, absence of heel, acres of deck space for sunbathing and the ability to make short, sharp coastal passages combine to make a multihull an attractive proposition. It rather depends how heavily an individual sailor rates the arguments against: vulnerability to damage in a crowded harbour, less all-round space below than a comparable monohull, the possibility of a higher insurance premium, and, last but not least, the slight amount of time required to set the boat up for trailing or launching.

5 The Rig

No matter how carefully calculated the form of the hull, if the design of the rig is defective, the boat will be a brute to handle in certain conditions, even if not perhaps in all. Admittedly, a good hull form will not be adversely affected as much as a cranky one but it may not be possible to deduce this from a single brief demonstration sail which is the most that can usually be hoped for before purchase.

The most widely encountered vices are, of course, lee and weather helm; both are hard on the temper – and arms – but the former is far and away the most unpleasant, even dangerous. The tendency to bear away uncontrollably, though bad enough in itself, is made more alarming by the acceleration as the boat's head falls away from the wind. Basically this is the result of too much sail area forward of the rig's centre of effort or too little hull area forward of the underbody's centre of lateral resistance: ie the headsail is too large or the keel is too far aft, the latter fault being rather more expensive to cure.

Weather helm, where the boat persistently heads up into wind, eventually luffing to a standstill, is caused by the opposite defects in design. It may be easier to remedy: by reducing mainsail area, sometimes simply by easing the traveller to leeward or, if there is a leech line fitted to the mainsail, freeing this off. In beamy boats with the rudder well aft, reducing the angle of heel so that the rudder is more deeply immersed should improve the situation. A degree of weather helm is usually tolerated as it gives some 'feel' to the helm; a boat which is in absolutely perfect balance can feel lifeless. Weather helm is occasionally also looked upon as something of a safety device, especially in dinghies and small keelboats: let go the tiller and the boat will immediately fly head to wind and stop there!

It does help if the sail area is appropriate to the size and purpose of the boat. The requirements of the racing enthusiast will obviously diverge from those of the cruising helmsman: when sailing competitively it is desirable to carry as much sail as possible. For those less preoccupied with this quest for speed, and whose crew is not made up of brawny

A nicely setting fractional rig on this Feeling 720 family trail sailer.

deck apes, the priority may simply be to reduce sail area as quickly and effortlessly as possible when needed.

With all trailer sailers, the length of the mast must also be a consideration, for two very good reasons. The first is that, when lashed on the deck for trailing, it must not project dangerously over the stern, and the second is that, obviously, the longer the spar, the more difficult it will be to raise and lower without assistance from a crane!

Ease of handling

Notwithstanding the unremitting search for innovative rigs – and some of the results of this search can best be described as bizarre – the Bermudian masthead sloop still is arguably the most suitable for a small, quick cruising boat. The mast, unless keel stepped, is not that much longer than the hull itself, both standing and running rigging are uncomplicated, the long headsail luff is efficient to windward and the working sail area, being almost equally divided between main and foresail is, in winds of up to 15 knots, well within the scope of a family crew. True, in a blow, the headsail will have to be exchanged for a smaller one, whereas in the case of a fractional rig with proportionally greater area in the mainsail it may be possible to avoid changing headsails with such frequency; except in very heavy going a tuck in the main will prevent overpowering but without unduly compromising balance.

Until fairly recently, swapping foresails or reducing their size was a precarious undertaking: struggling on an exposed and slippery foredeck for control of an acreage of slatting terylene would be further enlivened by blows about the ears from piston hanks, sheets and shackles. Alternative reefing methods do exist: the Wykeham Martin gear, forerunner of today's systems, which has been around for more than a half a century, proves both simple and trustworthy when employed in a small cruising boat with short luffed headsails. But it does have its limitations: when used in conjunction with a masthead Bermudian foresail the luff inevitably sags so far to leeward as to seriously impair windward performance, and without a tight luff the sail can become awkward to roll. Reef points are another way of tackling the problem – but just try tying a row in a force 5 wind over tide when the sail is flogging itself to death and fingers are numb! Quite apart from the physical exertion and risk of going over the side (neither lifelines nor safety harness should ever be looked upon as a guarantee of safety) the reefed sail, with its ungainly bundle of cloth lashed along the foot, will set deplorably and be all but useless on the wind. And there just could come a

Reefing a headsail on a slippery foredeck is one of the least attractive chores – and one reason for the increase in sales of headsail furling gear!

time when that last point gained to windward is all-important.

Today's headsail reefing systems have greatly improved the lot of the foredeck hand! Total control of the sail area calls for nothing more than an effortless tug of sheets or furling line, all from the security of the cockpit; no brawn required and no need for a drenching either. However, nothing is absolutely guaranteed to be foolproof. If a furling system does jam – and it can – this is all too often the result of its having been incorrectly set up. Should this occur, it is nonetheless rather an inconvenience. Infuriating it may be if a sail obstinately stays rolled up, but there are circumstances where the inability to furl it will place the vessel at risk. Not long ago, a multihull sailor to whom this did happen was off the Lizard, singlehanded at night – and in a gale. He was forced many miles off course, in fact, he sailed halfway around Britain! It made for a good yarn, but he was well aware how lucky it was that he had plenty of searoom – and plenty of stores!

There is another argument against headsail reefing on a small masthead Bermudian sloop and this is that the sail, even when completely furled, is responsible for a disproportionately large amount of windage which could be critical should the boat ever be faced with the need to run under 'bare' poles or lie a'hull. Few trailer sailers would be likely to encounter such weather in the course of normal coastal sailing, however, and the benefits would be considered to outweigh any slight risk brought about by fouled gear or an excess of windage.

In-mast mainsail reefing is promoted as the latest, greatest boon for the lightly crewed yacht. It certainly effects a speedy reduction in sail area, and with minimal exertion too, but at the time of writing, the mast (or luff spar if the system is retrofitted to an existing mast) is of necessity rather heavy in section. Neither is the equipment cheap and it might be hard to justify the cost on a mainsail area of much under 160 square feet. It must be admitted, though, that ever-smaller craft are finding it an attractive alternative to point, roller or slab reefing fitted to the boom. The mainsail often leaves something to be desired aerodynamically speaking and this despite the best efforts of the sailmakers. Since it is impracticable to fit horizontal battens it is not easy to build flow into the sail and a flat hollow-leeched triangle of terylene often results.

Fully-battened mainsails, adopted long ago by high performance multis, are at last being seen on many monohulls and not only those with a keen eye on performance. In spite of the high initial cost, not only of manufacturing the actual sail but also of the battens (a set of 5 for a 150 square foot mainsail wouldn't leave much change from £50 per set) it is perhaps surprising that full length battens have not been more in

The efficient fully-battened mainsail set by the Timpenny trail sailer.

favour. The rig has real benefits for the cruising yacht: both flogging and leech flutter are conspicuous by their absence under way and then too, the fully-battened mainsail is quick to lower and stow especially when restrained with lazy-jacks or twin topping lifts. With the long battens, the size of the roach can be increased allowing (for a given mast length) an increased area of sail high up and in clear air – and without an unsightly deep girt from the inner end of the battens to the clew as there otherwise might be. Nothing's perfect, however, and the battens, being less flexible than the fabric, can occasionally cause the sail, or part of it, to catch aback. This of course, makes it rather tricky to de-power the rig – always, it goes without saying, when an immaculate display of boat-handling is not only critical but also being scrutinised from the yacht club balcony. To avoid such humiliation, on larger boats, where muscle power alone might not flick the sail back into obedience, it is customary to fit roller batten cars rather than slides to the sail luff.

Classic revivals: gaffers and gunters

Gaff rig is enjoying a remarkable resurgence in popularity – not so much the massively sparred and hard-mouthed gaff rig as typified by the sailing trawlers, bawleys and pilot cutters, but a refined, rather whittled-down version, better balanced and easier for a family crew to manage. The interest in 'character' boats, where styling is based on that of their working ancestors, has produced some quite delightful small trailer sailers with effective workmanlike rigs set on relatively short, light spars.

The standing and running rigging, too, has in most cases been simplified and running backstays, one of the irritations generally associated with gaff rig (though not peculiar to it) have, wherever possible, been done away with. Not that running backstays are quite the deadly devices portrayed by popular myth: on the wind, they can simply be set up and left. It is when their presence is overlooked when gybing or attempting to bear away that they live up to their reputation for bringing downfall upon the crew. There have also been cases reported in backstays set up with a Highfield lever where injury has been inflicted as the arm snaps down – but then all items of a yacht's gear should be treated with respect. Now, when running backstays are fitted – as they are with some fractional and Bermudian cutter rigs – it is usual simply to tension them with a tackle and cam cleat.

To the purist, delighting in the sight of old gaffers storming along under a press of sail – jib topsails, jackyarders and watersails – the recent developments may look rather tame. They need not be. True, the sail areas may be smaller, booms shorter (the mainsail, in consequence, being far quicker to reef as and when necessary) and bowsprits less aggressive but it still takes a fair bit of skill to get the best from the rig. It is a powerful one, especially on a reach when the mainsail comes into its own, but a versatile rig with almost limitless combinations of sail possible, and its beauty, when everything is set to perfection, surely brings its own reward.

If there is a drawback to the gaff rig it may turn out to be the prosaic one of finance: when measuring for marina or harbour dues, officialdom is usually mean-spirited enough to run its tape along both bowsprit and bumpkin and levy charges accordingly. It may prove profitable to house both spars when in port! Trailing requirements will certainly mean that a projecting aft bumpkin, if fitted, will have to be detached before taking to the road and probably even a short bowsprit will have to be demounted, depending on whether or not it clears the tow vehicle.

Gunter rig, often confused with gaff, does in fact share most of the characteristics although the gaff is somewhat longer, usually lighter in section and is set vertically. Except on some Continental lake boats it is not greatly favoured by craft of any size although it could be said to combine the best points of Bermudian and gaff rigs: the high peaked mainsail is without question superior to windward than that of a conventional gaffer, the spars are short enough to stow on deck without overhang and the rig is quick and simple to set up even if it does share with its traditional predecessor the limitation of not being able to set a really large ghoster or spinnaker in light airs. Unfortunately, unlike a gaffer, a gunter yacht cannot make up for this deficiency by setting a topsail.

Cutters and yawls

The cutter rig, with two working headsails, is increasingly appreciated since the divided fore-triangle makes light work of sail handling. If the inner staysail is made of sufficiently heavy cloth, it can double as the storm jib. The inner forestay may be a source of mild annoyance if a large ghoster is set from the masthead since a crew member will need to be detailed to pass it around the stay when tacking, unless the stay is designed to be unclipped in light weather. All in all, though, it is a handy rig, in particular for cruising, as it is possible by correct trimming of the headsails (and some trial and error) to persuade many yachts to self-steer on some points of sailing.

The Rob Roy canoe yawl from Honnor marine, a delightful twenty-three footer with gunter mainsail and Bermudian mizzen.

Although the yawl rig enjoyed a vogue in the early years of this century (and once again in the ocean racers of the '60s where the diminutive mizzen was not measured for rating purposes) it is rarely seen on small yachts today. This said, nostalgia for the lovely designs of Albert Strange, not to mention the charismatic little canoe yawls of those distant days, has led to one or two designs being put into production. The best known must surely be the Drascombe lugger, even though it is essentially a dayboat with accommodation under a boom tent rather than a trailer sailer proper, but the builders, Honnor Marine, also introduced a few years back the beguiling 'Rob Roy' canoe yawl. This is a 23-footer based (loosely, it must be said) on the celebrated sailing canoe of the same name designed by John McGregor.

The yawl, by the way, is distinguished from the ketch by the position of the mizzen mast – in a yawl it is stepped aft of the rudder post. It is also usual for the mizzen of a ketch to be about one third of the area of the mainsail, whereas in a yawl it is a much smaller proportion. Too small, possibly, to produce any drive at all on the wind, it will anyway be back winded by the main when driving to windward as the yawl's mizzen will, in a boat of under 30 feet or so, be set on too short a mast to set a reaching staysail to good effect. This being the case, is the rig nothing less than a waste of effort, even though it looks attractive? Consider the added complications: another mast to step and rig (and the mizzen will almost certainly have to be sheeted to a bumpkin). The mast step also takes up cockpit or deck space – and there is the added cost, not only of spars and sail but also of rigging and cleats which must be allowed for. On the other hand, in a fresh breeze the boat will trundle along quite contentedly under foresail and mizzen and, in most cases even make to windward under this reduced sail area. The mizzen also keeps the boat head to wind – when fishing, for example – and can act as a steadying sail in an exposed anchorage. With the mizzen eased slightly and a small headsail aback, most small yachts will heave to quite peaceably – and this they might not do under influence only of main and jib.

The junk rig

If the idea of a labour-saving rig with a dash of originality appeals, then the Chinese lug or junk is worth more than a passing thought. To many, though not all, it is aesthetically pleasing and, when the sail is made from terylene and synthetics as opposed to the bamboo matting and superannuated fertiliser sacks seen among its Oriental cousins,it is quite functional! It may take a bit of getting to know but, once the strings are sorted, all sail handling can be carried out from the cockpit and there should be no need to venture on deck save in the unlikely event of an emergency.

Basically the sail is square in shape, varying according to the designer's preferences. It is fabricated from horizontal cloths, all flow being imparted by the external full length batten. These are adjusted by sheetlets leading to a single point on deck which control the leech so effectively that virtually all twist is eliminated. The sail always remains on the same side of the mast; on one tack the battens guard against distortion and chafe, while on the other the sail will fall away from the mast though it is fully controlled by the parrel lines. Reefing is just about instantaneous: on release of the halyard, the weight of the battens brings the sail down smoothly, like a Venetian blind, safely restrained by lazyjacks. Thanks to the

Fig 4 The rig.

a A fractional rigged Bermudian sloop. This type of rig, where the forestay does not extend to the mast truck is replacing the masthead rig as the favourite for both cruising and racing craft. The smaller fore-sail area is easier for light crews to man-age and there is no real need to invest in a comprehensive wardrobe of alternative headsails (in any case the fitting of roller furling gear claims to make them redun-dant). This rig is simply stayed, usually with one pair of lower shrouds and cap shrouds, a babystay, outer forestay, and standing backstay – though there may instead be two pairs of lower shrouds and no babystay. Depending on the degree to which the crew enjoy tweaking the rig, the backstay may be fitted with a tensioner in order to keep the headsail luff taut when sailing to windward and, in more highly tuned rigs, to induce a certain amount of mast bend and so flattening the mainsail.

b A high aspect and very powerful rig for a fast cruising trailable catamaran. The large mainsail with full-length battens supports a very heavy roach, developing a lot of drive on a reach. The battens not only make it possible to add extra area in the upper portion of the sail, where it is most useful, but prevent it from flogging and also assist quick stowage since the cloth is under control at all times. The small headsail can be rigged so as to be self-acting. A larger sail can be set in light airs, though light multihulls are so easily driven that there is little chance to set a ghoster or spinnaker; little need either if it comes to that!

c A gunter yawl – or should it be ketch as the mast is in fact stepped forward of the rudder? The high-peaked gunter rig is regarded as markedly superior to the traditional gaff when it comes to making up to windward yet, with one or two notable exceptions, it is only rarely set – in Britain at least. In Europe many of the lake sailing types have accepted and refined it, often setting fully battened heavily roached mainsails on a curved yard. But in the form shown in the sketch it is quite a pleasant easy-going rig for a cruising boat since it is possible to potter along happily under only the main and self-tacking staysail. Here the staysail is shown attached to a 'Peter boom', where the fore end of the boom is made fast to deck swivel which allows the sail to take up the correct camber when running downwind. On the other hand, given the appropriate conditions, performance can be pepped up by setting both headsails, the mizzen and a light mizzen staysail into the bargain! True, the tiny mizzen contributes little if anything to performance on the wind, but it does ensure the boat will always keep its head up; it is also a handy steadying sail when motoring and will keep the boat lying head to wind in a choppy anchorage. It is a useful rig for a trailsailer, as no spars are longer than the hull and all can be lightly constructed. Sometimes both gaff and boom are hollow to further reduce weight.

d James Wharram's low aspect gaff wingsail with short gaff and wraparound mainsail luff. The mainsail is loose-footed and the sheet leads from a clew board to a rope horse aft.

Fig 4 Continued.

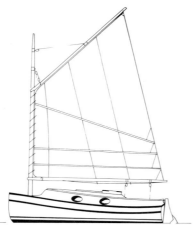

e A version (somewhat tamed) of an
American cat boat. This breed sets an
enormous – usually gaff – mainsail on an
unstayed mast. Although the rig enjoys a
certain vogue in Britain amongst some
traditionalists, it is not happiest in strong
winds and rough water; the long boom
makes it laborious tying in a reef (roller
reefing would be impractical) and the
mast weight tends to put the boat's head
under, buoyant though the forward sections are. On a run, without a foresail to
provide an element of balance, this type
of rig is very prone to roll heavily. On a
reach though, the rig asserts itself – the
large undivided sail area pushes the hull
along at the maximum waterline length
with no need for the complications of
cruising chutes or genoa.

f A cat ketch – although it could reasonably
be argued that it should be termed a
schooner since both the unstayed masts
are of equal length. In theory the rig is
ideal for a family-crewed trailer sailer: it is
self-tacking, can be reefed without leaving the cockpit (in fact, to some extent it is
self-reefing since the masts are very flexible and spill wind in a gust) and the encircling wishbone booms are too light to
inflict serious damage to an unwary head
in the event of an unexpected gybe. In
light airs it does suffer a lack of sail area,
but with care, it is possible to set watersails under the boom or fly a ghoster set
on a sacrificial halyard: this will part in
any violent gust which might otherwise
carry away the mast. Reefing, although
easy enough, requires a good deal of
experimentation to acquire a successful
rig balance; sailing under either main or
foresail alone results in a loss of control.
And, when reefed, the bundle sail creates
undesirable windage. One plus point is
that the masts are quick to step and lower
– so long as the technique has been
perfected.

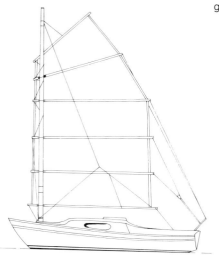

g The Chinese lug, or as it is more usually known, junk rig. This has acquired an almost mystical aura from its early association with the famous long distance single handed races where managability and prudence were the keynotes. Now that there is big prize money to be fought for in such publicised events as the Round Britain and the Trans-ocean short-handed races, it has been revealed that a single crew member can manage a vast acreage of sail set on a conventional, if sophisticated, Bermudian rig, which may have resulted in a downturn in enthusiasm for junk rig! Nevertheless, it does have a lot to offer when cruising, though it is perhaps least efficacious on the smaller boat where the cost, weight of the mast (and difficulty in stepping and lowering it without outside assistance even where the spar is hinged above deck level) and windage of the reefed sail rather outweigh any advantage gained from being able to handle the sail entirely from the cockpit. And even this is negated when the gear fails or a sheetlet snarls as it may well do. The choice may in the end boil down to personal preference. Undoubtedly there is a slight performance drop at either end of the Beaufort scale – but this may not be noticeable to the cruising skipper – even if it may not be the first priority.

h Standing lug (as opposed to 'dipping lug' where the mainsail has to be lowered to come about – then re-set). This is a powerful rig when correctly set up but halyard and tack downhaul tension are critical.

battens, the unreefed area of sail retains its shape perfectly. There is never any flogging and very little risk of the sail shredding itself even in the worst weather; if a rip should start, it will be limited to the single cloth bounded by its particular batten.

Whether it is the perfect rig for a very small yacht is open to debate. Undoubtedly the 19-foot Newbridge Navigator sails very handily with it, though this particular design has full sections forward, a desirable feature as the unstayed and flexible mast is quite heavy and could cause a finer-lined yacht to bury the bow. The cost of the rig is comparable to that of a conventional sloop whose sail wardrobe would consist not only of the working sails, but also storm jib, genoa and spinnaker – redundant with the junk! The substantial keel-stepped mast is expensive, admittedly – though the price differential is almost negated by the absence of winches, blocks and other sail-handling apparatus, none of which are necessary on the small junk-rigged boat. True, without a ghoster, light air sailing might be seem rather lacklustre and there would be those who might find that boring. But it is not out of the question to set a light headsail, though only on a sacrificial halyard which would part in a gust, before the mast could suffer damage from a strain for which it was not intended. But this would seem to defeat the prime virtue of the rig – its simplicity.

Accepting that, in medium to fresh winds, performance is not markedly inferior to a Bermudian sloop, are there any snags inherent in the rig which would render it impracticable for a trailer sailer?

Well, that hefty mast could well be construed as a snag since it would ordinarily need the services of a crane in order to step or un-ship it! One solution which Newbridge boats came up with is to hinge the mast about four feet above the deck. Once the long upper section is lowered the entire spar becomes quite easy to manhandle. But the biggest drawback to my mind is one which is really only applicable to the small yacht and it is simply that of windage: windage of the foot of the partly reefed sail which is considerable, introducing a marked increase in leeway – and knifing to windward is not in any case the strong suit of the Chinese lug rig. Even with the sail lowered and secured on its gallows, it remains quite an unwieldy bundle, one which can make motoring in cross winds very tricky; it also induces rolling at anchor and, in anything of a blow it would pay to stow the sail on deck –

which is a time-consuming task and so, to some extent, self-defeating. But there is undoubtedly a place for this rig. On a yacht over 25 feet or so it really comes into its own, in particular for long-distance, short-handed voyaging. Here, anything that helps to lessen crew fatigue and exposure can only increase safety margins. For a trailer sailer, especially one at the smaller end of the scale, it might be less than ideal.

The wishbone rig

Mention a wishbone schooner and thoughts drift to a tall-masted superyacht with clipper bows, trail boards and sparkling brightwork, clouds of white canvas spread to the north-east Trades. Certainly a trailer sailer would not immediately spring to mind! But the truth is that a two-masted rig where the sails are set on – or rather within – encircling wishbone booms (in the manner of a sailboard) cannot really be described as anything but a wishbone schooner – the masts are, after all, of identical height. It is not a rig much in evidence although the 22-foot Poacher, a flush-decked lift keel tearaway, exploited it with some success; this little trailer sailer was in production for several years and I confess to having been sufficiently taken with the concept to buy one! The rig, a variation on what is now referred to as the Freedom rig, had both good and bad points: it pointed acceptably high and, in a breeze, was very quick downwind; like the junk rig, however, it suffered from a lack of sail area in light airs. I did risk setting a cruising chute when the occasion seemed to merit it (with some trepidation and a halyard designed to fail-safe); I also experimented with watersails under the booms, and every inch helped! The rig is simple in principle but the sails need to be cut with some precision. Neither should they be over-full as the flow is adjusted easily by clew tension. The luffs of the foresail and main (there are no jibs) are sleeved around the unstayed keel-stepped masts. These masts taper markedly from deck to truck and are remarkably flexible, spilling wind in a blow and so, to some extent, making the rig self-reefing in squally conditions. For the length, each mast is very light in weight and two people can step one without much difficulty even if the operation does call for a bit of confidence: the first attempt can be unnerving as the spar teeters on its balance point. But

The gas cutter rig of this Skanner 19 is both pretty and easy to handle – if a bit short of area for light winds,

practice makes perfect and it is possible to step the mast in a couple of minutes (all the time keeping a wary eye out for unexpected gusts of wind!)

Each sail is controlled by a single sheet and needs no adjustment when tacking. In the event of a sudden squall, the mainsail can be lowered quickly but ideally the sails should be progressively reduced in area, an operation which can be carried out from the cockpit although a fair lead from clew to turning blocks on the mast is critical. With a light boat the rig is actually more sensitive to balance than might be supposed and a few trial outings are advisable in order to establish the best practice. But the absence of flogging, the self-tacking factor, and the lack of booms to crack unwary skulls in an unplanned gybe, all of these are plus points for those who sail with a young or inexperienced crew.

The Liberty, a 23-foot David Thomas design, exploits a similar idea in that the masts are unstayed and flexible, though they hinge for easier lowering. The boat is actually ketch-rigged, like the Poacher without head sails and, like the Poacher, committed to keeping the sail controls to a bare minimum. Instead of wishbone booms the designer opted for more conventional spars supporting loose-footed sails. The builders, Hunter Boats, describe the Liberty as a cat ketch, this being in deference to the well-known North American cat boats. These sport a single unstayed mast forward with a gaff-rigged mainsail – and, in spite of a tendency to dig the bows in when the going is choppy, perform surprisingly well to windward: on a reach they power along superbly; on a dead run, the long heavy boom makes them roll like the devil. It says much for the inherent masochism of those who sail them that they remain the object of so much veneration.

Many are the ways of harnessing the power of the winds and no matter how off-beat a few of the 'modern' ones may appear, the majority have been experimented with before in one form or another. The technology is better nowadays and there is perhaps more interchange of ideas and experiences between owners. But you have only to thumb through the yachting publications of the last century to see accounts of sky-scraping, rule-cheating rigs, even if these were not as a rule, aimed at the short-handed skipper; after all, labour was cheap and without the demand for paid hands, the south and east coast fisherman would have had a lean time of it during the summer months: hauling sheets was far more profitable than hauling nets!

Some of the more recherché rigs were amazingly effective, at least on some points of sailing. Among these could be numbered the Lungström or Lapwing rig which spread on double booms off the wind and folded, sail on sail, when sailing on the wind. Trials have been carried out with hockey stick masts, bipod masts, to say nothing of kites: all of these have proved to have some advantages some of the time. As all-round performers, though, most failed abysmally. And it is as an all-round performer that the rig of a trailer sailer should be judged, at least in the first instance.

6 Buying a Boat

The purchase of a new yacht is straightforward enough; whether or not it is sensible can be debatable if looked at purely from the financial angle. Unlike a car a boat may not depreciate dramatically the instant it leaves the showroom, but the value does drop even when the vessel remains in pristine condition. Over the years, certain classes may appear to have held their prices, perhaps even increased in value, but this is illusory; take into account the real purchasing power of the cash and, over a 10-year period, the depreciation is marked. The anticipatory delight of actually ordering the boat, brand-new and shrink-wrapped, is all very well but this does wear off all too quickly; expectations of a new boat are high, it must be perfect in all respects. Sadly, this will not invariably be the case; teething troubles do occur and, although it is incumbent upon the supplier to rectify any defects within a specified period of time, any problem with a new boat is most disheartening.

It is also quite possible to purchase a boat and a trailer second-hand for a very modest outlay; the market is usually buoyant and there are bargains to be had.

That said, the buying of a second-hand boat of whatever age can be beset with pitfalls. The only sensible advice is to have the boat professionally surveyed. Depending upon the age of the boat this will, in any case, be unavoidable in order to get insurance. Companies vary in their demands; fifteen years is the usual age at which a structural survey is mandatory, but ten or even five years are not unheard of. This should be undertaken by a surveyor known or recommended to you and with experience in the type of boat in question; it may not be in your interest to employ one suggested by the vendor. The usual purchase procedure is to make a deposit of ten per cent of the purchase price, subject to survey, this being refundable if any major structural defects are revealed. Recommendations (if any) contained within the report will have to be implemented in full and this will naturally affect negotiations. Whilst a recent survey made out to a third party (ie the vendor or agent) will, in many instances, be sufficient to arrange insurance or finance for the vessel – so long as the surveyor is acceptable to the company concerned – it does not offer any redress should faults be discovered. The report must be addressed specifically to you.

The employment of surveyors does not come cheap. If there are found to be serious defects in a vessel, the cost of a survey may be saved several times over but, on the other hand the fee is unlikely to be waived just because, on close inspection, the boat involved turns out to be beyond human aid. Bearing this in mind, it may help a prospective purchaser if he or she can manage a certain amount of preliminary fault-finding before calling in a surveyor.

Establishing priorities

Before assessing the vessel's structural state a buyer should have his priorities established. The first of these must be that the boat can safely be trailed behind the intended tow vehicle – the combined weight of boat and trailer should not exceed the kerb weight of the car – and this is where a purpose-built trailer sailer will score over a less specialised design. Not that this necessarily excludes those yachts where lightness of construction is not the first consideration, even

A Falmouth Bass Boat. Open camping boats such as this can be trailed behind the smallest car and are rewarding to sail as well as reasonably priced.

though such a boat will almost certainly be shorter and offer less accommodation for its weight and price.

High performance might also rate high on the list of desirable, even essential attributes. In certain areas, there may be keen racing for a club's adopted one-design class and such versatile examples as the Sonata and E-boat, sporty enough when it comes to thrashing round the buoys, are also quite at home on a more leisurely coastal cruise. Most light displacement yachts are quite lively to handle, though the inexperienced should be chary of purchasing a one-off built specifically for racing and for nothing else. On the face of it, some of these mini and quarter-tonners, with wide beam and light, rakish hulls (albeit with high aspect fixed fin keel on the underside) seem at first glance to offer a lot of boat for little outlay. Rudimentary as the interior fittings tend to be, it is no difficult matter to fit a galley and instal berths. But these craft can be rather fragile, as they were usually built with a limited lifespan in mind, perhaps only three or four seasons' racing. On occasion the concept might prove successful enough to instigate a production run – once the snags of the prototype had been ironed out. While many of these boats are drawn by well-known designers, this is not always so; amateurs can, and do, produce first-rate boats, but their failures can be spectacular and the trouble is, by the time the vices of the boat are revealed, it may be too late to do much about it.

The type of keel will be determined by the boat's intended sailing waters and whether it is to be left for long periods on a half-tide mooring; in both cases either bilge keels or a flush bottom with lift keel or plate would probably be favoured. The number of overland excursions planned should also be taken into account, as should the facilities available at launching sites: the majority of boatyards and marinas have at least one slip from which a deep fin keel boat could be launched, something that would be difficult, if not actually impossible, from a shallow beach or slip without considerable rise and fall of tide. That deep fin can make life difficult for the crew camping on board on land as well: it will be a scramble up to the deck which youngsters might even find impossible.

Accommodation, when all is said and done, is mainly based upon the usual number of crew and their collective stoicism! But the space and luxury, or otherwise, of the interior does explain the wide variations in price between different designs with similar overall length.

Outboard or inboard?

There is yet another factor which has a marked influence on price, even between boats of the same class. This is the type of auxiliary engine, whether it is an inboard or outboard. If an inboard is considered absolutely essential, certain types of trailer sailer can be ruled out at one stroke since the installation in a completely flush-bottomed boat is not recommended: in the absence of even a vestigial keel or skeg, there is no protection whatever for the shaft, bracket and propeller, so these will be very vulnerable to damage during the launch or recovery – to say nothing of risks incurred in the event of grounding. Besides, the benefit of this hull configuration is wiped out if sterngear projects through it. The size of the boat might also mitigate against an inboard installation – certainly a diesel, even a modern single-cylinder model, would occupy an undue amount of space in a boat under 20 feet overall.

Outboard auxiliaries have the reputation for being something of a mixed blessing: oily, unreliable, an extra weight carried where it is least wanted – right on the transom – and largely ineffective in a seaway since the motion repeatedly flings the propeller clear of the water. Bad reputations take

A nicely designed outboard well

quite a while to live down but it is fair to say that today's small outboard is clean running and, if well maintained, can usually be counted on to start – and run – on demand. Power to weight ratios are better too, so that the weight right aft has hardly any adverse effect on the trim of even the smallest boat. True, the transom-mounted outboard does not perform to great advantage in waves and really the only way to overcome this is to instal it in a cockpit well; here it will be tucked in under the hull and remain immersed even in severe pitching. Early experiments were not particularly successful due in part to the oil-rich fuel mixture and the fumes it created, but the lower oil content of the two-stroke mix used in modern machines has helped to overcome this problem.

The saildrive combines inboard and outboard and, since the shaft and sterngear is contained within a single faired leg projecting through the underbody, the siting of the engine is less critical. But, as with a conventional shaft installation, it is best suited to an underbody whose form offers some protection when grounding.

Unloved though it may be by purists who dislike and distrust any motive power save wind and muscle, some form of auxiliary motor is really indispensable in these days of highly organised leisure and working hours. But an engine may be more than the means of creeping home long after the tide has turned and the wind breathed its last; an alternator or lighting coil fitted to it will also charge the battery and so power navigation and domestic lighting, instruments and of course, also start the engine. And though a 40 amp/hour 12-volt battery may well suffice to run a couple of cabin lights for an average season, little else can be expected of it unless there is some means of charging.

The more complicated the engine and the systems, the more there is to go wrong – simplicity once again may prove to be the best policy. Even with older boats, where components are fairly accessible, fault-finding can be an exhausting undertaking; in a GRP yacht with moulded internal fitments, it is worse by far (and removal of an inboard may require really drastic surgery to cockpit and bridgedeck). Even so, problems can, almost without exception, be rectified. Damage or deterioration of the hull structure itself might be a different story for there are certain defects which are economic to repair. Both glassfibre and wood are susceptible to ailments in the same places and from similar causes.

Wooden craft

If buying a timber trailer sailer the chances are high that it will be built of veneer, either moulded or in the form of sheet ply. Both methods of construction are tough, light and, when in a sound state, resilient enough to withstand the stresses imposed by regular trailing. However, a boat of traditional plank on frame type, either with clinker or carvel strakes, is most unhappy out of its natural element. The wood dries out and is liable to shrink and split along the length; any caulking may be affected and fastenings be loosened by the movement of the trailer.

A plywood hull will in most instances be of single or double chine type (with one or more sharp angles at the turn of the bilge). It may be professionally built, or constructed from a prefabricated kit or set of drawings – there is even the possibility that it is the end product of a cigarette packet sketch! Although there are a dozen well-documented small cruiser classes dating from the early '60s whose length and weight make them suitable candidates for trailer sailing, not all can be identified with certainty if only because minor alterations, to windows, coachroof length (and height) and even hull profile, may have been made either at the time of build or during the lifespan. So unless you are certain, and there is a known history, it is best to proceed on the basis that what you see is what you get and accept the boat as a type rather than a class.

This approach is also sensible when it comes to assessing the construction and likely defects. Do not assume that the vessel has in fact been built by yard or factory: look for evidence of poor workmanship in butt joints, where the ply panels lap against each other, backed up by a timber strap. Suspect the bilge stringers, where inaccurate chamfering may have been packed out with glue and sawdust. Don't forget to have a close look at bulkheads and ensure that they have not come away from the hull skin at any point (or to be precise, that this skin has not parted company from them since many hulls were built upside-down over bulkhead-formers which remained in place, only a few ultra-light boats having the building bulkheads removed afterwards). The absence of these common faults is in itself encouraging as it does suggest that boat was soundly constructed at the outset.

Delamination of the veneers is the most widespread – and

potentially fatal – disease of the plywood boat (and it is one which affects both hot and cold moulded hulls too). Unless a determined attempt has been made to circumvent water penetration of the end grain – and this may be achieved by a generous glue line, sealing with epoxy or polyester resin or, on exposed areas such as hatch tops and cockpit benches, cleating exposed edges with timber slips, some breakdown of the veneers is almost inevitable with the passing of the years. It is, unfortunately, quite easy to hide evidence of this beneath layers of stopping and paint. Unless this attempt has been made, it will be visible initially in the form of narrow ridges running the way of the surface grain – these indicate that the upper veneer has separated from the glue line and adjoining timber. More water will find its way in, expand and split the ridges open; the process accelerates, affecting the underlying veneers and, in the end, destroying the plywood.

In the case of a chine yacht, with almost vertical topsides and little or no compound curvature to confuse the issue, it is sometimes possible to make out areas which have deteriorated and been subsequently touched up: suspect any undulations in the skin, or sections where the surface is smoother than that in the immediate vicinity due to the presence of filler. All types of filler will, if heavily applied, sound slightly deader than the surrounding ply when tapped with the knuckles.

Moulded veneer

Where the boat in question is of round-bilge moulded veneer construction, the delamination can be very difficult indeed to detect but regrettably, if the boat is more than a few seasons old, it will almost invariably be present to a greater or lesser degree. This, surprisingly perhaps, holds true for professionally-built craft as well as the handful of yachts which have been moulded by amateurs. As with as all delamination, it is brought about by the action of damp and, although theoretically, with a homogeneous structure such as a moulded hull, water permeation is impossible, in practice this has proved not to be the case. During the building process, the veneers are laid up over a mould and each layer is stapled to the one preceding, the staples then being removed and the holes filled. On occasion, this operation is not carried out as meticulously as it should be, and either a few staples remain *in situ*

– where they eventually corrode away to allow water to carry on its insidious work – or the holes are overlooked with the same end result. Damp may also find its way into the hull through corroded fastenings or fittings, and many early cold-moulded boats had ribs inserted after the skin was laid up; these are especially prone to suffer from wet rot and/or delamination.

To some extent, defects could be said to have been inbuilt although this would not have been suspected at the time. The resin glues developed during the late forties were immensely strong and reasonably tolerant of temperature fluctuations, but on occasions the mixing may have been less than thorough, the glue spread with a careless hand or the atmosphere just too cold to allow a perfect cure (I have also seen a case where the glue clearly set too rapidly, before the next veneer skin could be stapled into place, and this resulted in alarming and widespread voids).

Hot-moulded boats, where the temperature was rigidly controlled during building, are generally less seriously affected by delamination since the glue line cured uniformly. But in neither type of moulded hull are signs of delamination, in particular of major internal voids, easy to spot. Methodical tapping of stressed areas such as the turn of the bilge and garboard tuck may reveal that all is not well, but in the majority of instances all that may be visible are cracks or a slight curl along the veneer strips. Determined efforts may have been made to fair these – the usual procedure being first to mount an assault with a power sander followed by a cover operation with lavish distribution of glassfibre paste. It is not unknown for much of one or even more of the veneer skins to be severely eroded by unskilled use of a sander, but the extent of damage will only be revealed by stripping down the hull which may not be possible before purchase. Repairs of this nature are seldom, if ever, worthwhile over the long term; correct remedial action is vital and should only be attempted by a shipwright, and a good one at that, if the structural integrity of the hull is to be preserved.

Admittedly, there are not many moulded small cruisers around which can be happily towed by a family car, if one-off racing boats are excluded. But, examples of the Fairey Atalanta, a 26-foot centre cockpit sloop with lifting bilge keels are quite common. This particular craft was specifically designed 40 years ago as a trailer sailer and is now regarded as a classic – as is the rather prettier 23-foot centreplate

Audacity, designed by Laurent Giles. Both the Illingworth and Primrose Top Hat and Robert Tucker's Ariel, each around 25 foot overall could be trailed behind a powerful car, though both are fixed keel boats, albeit of moderate draft. There are even smaller craft as well, but moulded ply was one of the more expensive forms of construction and was used, in the main, to produce bespoke craft. The use of the new wonder material, glass reinforced plastic (GRP) had superseded moulding in timber by the early '60s.

If damage brought about by collision or grounding is discounted, hull faults in wooden yachts are nearly always directly attributable to the arch-enemy of wood – water! Water can and will insinuate itself through just about any timber joint or through-hull fastening. This being the case, the chainplates, floors – or stringers – through which keel bolts pass, and any woodwork in the way of deck fittings, should be examined with a suspicious eye, and gently poked with the flat edge of a chisel if doubt exists. The very nails, screws and bolts keeping a timber hull together are also a prime site for water ingress and, if these have corroded, the wood through which they pass will decay, and create an expensive task for a shipwright once again. The effects of stress should not be ignored either – much of this is the result of inadequate mast compression support. In a boat built from sheet ply, the main evidence of this may be in a flattened camber to deck or coachroof (depending where the mast is stepped) and possibly, discernible movement of the chainplate bolts or deck eyes; in a moulded boat, the veneers may actually have opened and this will be visible along external glue lines. The seams of a carvel, clinker or strip-planked boat will almost certainly suffer some distortion as may the sheerline.

Glassfibre

Glassfibre hulls are not immune to water penetration. Indeed, water is directly responsible for the affliction that strikes terror into the heart of the would-be purchaser – osmosis! Osmosis is actually the name of the process by which blisters in the gel – and sometimes in the underlying laminate – are formed, rather than the term for the damage itself. It might seem unlikely that moisture is able to work its way into a seamless hull but it does and this, in the great majority of cases, is simply because no resin so far developed has proved to be one hundred per cent impervious to water, although modern isophtalic and epoxy resins do come pretty close. But there are instances where the blame can be attributed to poor temperature and ambience control during lamination – even to the use of a mould which has, for whatever reason, been allowed to become excessively cold or damp.

Once water has insinuated itself through the outer gelcoat, it leaches away at the chemicals of the resin binding the glass cloth and mat, eventually expanding to form the characteristic blisters associated with 'osmosis'. Unpleasant as these may appear (and a bad case really does look much like the proverbial 'boat pox') it is often neither so widespread nor so immediately threatening as it is held to be.

In view of the high cost of remedial action when carried out by a specialist firm, even a handful of blisters does constitute ammunition in any battle over price. Localised patches of blistering are easy enough for an amateur to cope with, by grinding out affected areas, drying the hull (which may be easier said than done, even when the underbody is tented) and filling and fairing to the chemical manufacturer's specifications. There is, of course, no guarantee that other blisters will not appear but they can be dealt with as an ongoing maintenance problem rather than as candidates for emergency surgery. A severe case, where over ten per cent of the underbody is affected is another matter, and will almost certainly entail a complete programme of gelcoat blasting or peeling, drying of the laminate and re-application of gel under controlled conditions. In a small boat the cost may not be justified on economic grounds.

Fortunately, gelcoat blistering is not usually difficult to spot so long as there is not a heavy build-up of antifouling (and the hull has been cleaned of weed and slime prior to the inspection). It is a good idea to look closely at the hull more than once: as the sun moves, shadows will vary and may throw blisters, invisible from one angle, into high relief. The sense of touch too plays an important part, as small blisters can sometimes be felt when they cannot be seen.

Delamination is altogether more serious and far more difficult to detect. A moisture meter may reveal liquid filled areas, but over a period of time these may have dried out, leaving dry voids. On deck, if the core material – usually, though not invariably – balsa or foam (for lightness) has separated from th resin, movement may be felt and there may be a tell-tale creaking sensation underfoot. Delamination of the hull lay-up

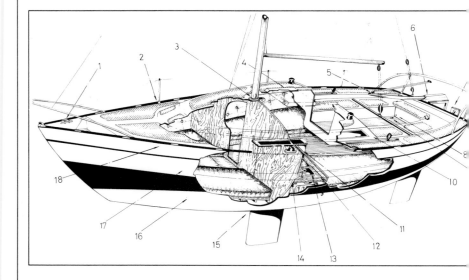

Fig 5

The boat in this cut-away drawing is representative of a type of trailer sailer rather than of any individual boat. Although most of the faults to be looked out for are endemic to glassfibre, wooden boats are, in the main, subject to problems at similar points on the hull, deck and general structure.

Check all stress areas closely for signs of crazing or cracking. There may be internal damage to decks even if no external signs are in evidence. Damage will sometimes be revealed by laying a heavy straightedge across a section; if not completely level there is a possibility that delamination may have started within the layers of cloth or internal foam. Therefore examine with care:

1 All cleats, in particular mooring cleats, and look under the deck to see they have adequate backing plates and that fastenings are sound.

2 All other deck fittings: stanchion sockets are vulnerable to damage and in some designs are also very poorly attached so that the inevitable movement will ultimately damage the deck itself. Examine deck eye shroud attachments; make absolutely certain that where these are fitted the load is distributed to an internal bulkhead or brace – occasionally this is not the case, with results which can be imagined!

3 Around the mast heel – be especially chary of horizontal crazes extending across the deck.'Incidents' the rather euphemistic word used to describe virtually all disasters at sea, rarely come about from a breakdown of the hull structure but are usually brought about by failure of minor components or one or more of the yacht's mechanical – or domestic – systems. So, keeping this in mind:

4 Check the condition of hatch and flushing boards – all should be watertight and also capable of being secured (and opened) from within. There should also be a means of keeping the flushing boards in place in the unlikely event of a capsize.

5 Make certain the tiller, if of timber, is not delaminating and that an extension, if fitted, has a universal joint.

6 See that both rudder blade and head are sound and that the rudder can lift or pivot freely. Examine all gudgeons and pintles for signs of wear, corrosion or crazing in the adjacent laminate or timber.

7 The outboard bracket should lift easily and be mounted at the correct height for the outboard used with it – which may not be the case if the outboard is a different model from that originally recommended for the boat. Look for stress crazing around the mounting bolts.

8 The gas bottle must be connected to the appliance and conform with current regulations. All hoses and clips must be in perfect condition and the bottle must be securely contained within a separate gas-tight locker fitted with an overside drain. All cockpit lockers should be fitted with a means of secure retention – and at least one should lock. Make certain, in the case of a deep sidebench locker, that it is not possible for water to drain directly into the main bilge.

9 Where the cockpit drains pass through the underbody they should be fitted with seacocks.

10 Check the windows for leaks, damage to frames and crazing or cracking of acrylic panes. This is common on the fastenings which should, incidentally, be through bolts *not* self-tapping screws! Also look out for cracks in the coachroof adjacent to windows; this would suggest stress.

11 Examine the lift-keel box (or centreplate case) for signs of wringing or seepage; pay careful attention to the lower edges.

12 If there is no forehatch fitted, the galley should *not* be sited immediately adjacent to the main hatch which would form the sole means of escape in the event of fire.

13 Unless the sink discharges well above the waterline, it must be fitted with a gate valve.Structural damage or deterioration to the hull can usually be rectified – but this may be a costly undertaking. And though a boat is well prepared and polished for sale, there may be hidden defects which a meticulous inspection may bring to light. So:

14 Examine all load bearing bulkheads for movement where they are joined to the hull moulding.

15′ Check the underbody carefully for evidence of damage due to grounding, whether that grounding has been a once-only unintentional matter or has occurred more gently but over a longer period of time spent on a drying mooring!

16 Peer closely at the underbody of a glassfibre boat for the dreaded blisters: even the smallest are usually visible even through the antifouling. They should not necessarily constitute a bar to the purchase of the boat, although they are a handy negotiating factor. Unless the blistering is severe with roughly ten per cent or more of the underbody affected, it is generally possible to carry out remedial work yourself, although it takes time and the affected areas must be thoroughly dried.

17 Examine all areas for signs of crazing which will usually indicate a previous encounter with an unyielding object. Crazing can be obscured by paint but not for long!

18 If there are signs of mastic extruding from the toerail joint, this suggests that there has been a problem with the join. Examine the through bolts internally.

does tend to take place mainly as a result of impact damage or running ground but usually there will also be some additional evidence pointing to such an occurrence.

If the cause of structural problems associated with the glassfibre hull is well known, accurate prediction of potential trouble spots still does not seem possible. Even with boats of the same class, produced by the same yard to an identical specification, one boat may suffer severe eruptions of the gelcoat while the sister ship may remain as perfect as when first launched. Rumours are current as to which yachts – and from which builders – suffer more than their fair crop of blisters, but there are so many variables (not least among these being whether the craft spends its time in warm waters or cold, fresh or saline, and also whether it is laid up ashore for part of the year) that it is best to consider each only on the specific evidence presented.

Common problems

Cracks or crazing of hull or deck should be looked upon with the disfavour accorded to blisters – while not all that serious in themselves, depending of course upon the extent and location – they do tend to be indicative of either an underlying stress problem or of previous damage. Cracks in resin-rich areas such as the inner edges of toerails or curved cockpit corners may be only the result of slight shrinkage of the gel and as such, can be disregarded as they don't impair the structural integrity of the moulding. Others though, may justify more specific investigation, in order to remove not merely the symptom but also the original cause.

The most common single site of crazing due to stress is around stanchion bases and this, if not caused by collision, is the result of ill-considered design; few fittings on a boat would seem to be subjected to as much trial and error as stanchion sockets (which are, after all, subject to a heavy and sudden loading should a selfish crew member, en route overboard, grab at a stanchion in extremis!). The only permanent cure is to re-fix the socket, possibly with a heavier backing pad but, depending upon interior linings, this can be a long and awkward job. All crazes around fittings, in particular those adjacent to chainplates and deck eyes, should give rise to concern and the internal bolts, backings and/or braces be scrutinised. These, by the way, may turn out to be less than substantial and may even be conspicuous by their absence!

Crazing around windows is clear evidence of undue flexing and in the case of through hull windows, which are subjected to occasional immersion, it may eventually prove a source of real problems with the surrounding laminates. If it is in the way of the mast step or tabernacle it may be indicative of problems caused by compression stress. It is never easy to judge accurately whether the cracks appeared within the first season or two and never subsequently worsened or whether, unless the internal stiffening is strengthened, the area will continue to deteriorate. In any event, such crazing provides a strong incentive to re-negotiate the asking price.

According to the size and severity of any crazes – and the light level at the time of the examination – they sometimes remain undetected and minor ones can be obliterated with light filler and paint. Hairline cracks, although not invariably of great structural significance, can be polished to the point where they are only discernible in strong sunlight – or with the aid of a fluorescent hand lantern. But, unless subjected to a complete programme of grinding back, filling and fairing, crazes will not stay hidden for long since the surface of the gelcoat will move, albeit very slightly, and a painted area will open up along the original craze lines. Small areas of star cracks on the topsides may be the result of a hard spot – perhaps an interior fitment which has prevented uniform flexing of the hull, but are far more likely to be the result of something as prosaic as a close encounter with a harbour wall or other similarly unyielding object; neither is it unheard of for boats to slip off trailers during launch or recovery. If a hull has longitudinal cracks, suspect the likelihood of internal damage. Confirmation of this may only be possible after stripping out part of the fixtures and fittings. This preoccupation with what is on the surface only a minor blemish may sound alarmist, but crazes allow water to penetrate the gel and, eventually, the substrate as well. Going over the affected area with a moisture meter may produce astonishingly high readings, and it must never be forgotten that it is moisture which will ultimately lead to voids and delamination.

The keel, or rather the joint between keel and hull, provides a constant source of inspiration and delight to the surveyor who can otherwise find no faults! Unless keels are encapsulated, as they are with the majority of modern glassfibre yachts, there are bolts to corrode, weaken and leak. Even low aspect external keels are vulnerable to the accepted hazards of maritime life. Centreline and bilge keels are susceptible to injuries after grounding; these include wringing, movement and occasionally, summary removal. Steel-plate bilge keels rust but when replacement is needed (and this is not an unduly onerous task) it is self-evident. Weeps along the upper edge of the keel should be taken as a sign that all is not well, as too should layers of freshly trowelled mastic. Otherwise the true extent of any defect may not necessarily show up at first glance. Slight buckling in the hull, fore or aft of the keel root, might be noticed, which would suggest a former brief encounter with a submerged obstacle. There may be crazing in the glassfibre hull adjoining the keel: this, as can well be imagined, could have sinister implications. On the other hand, in the case of a lightly-built racing boat, it is customary to fair over the hull/keel join with filler; this filler tends to shrink or flex and will therefore crack during the season; replacement is accepted as a routine part of the annual maintenance programme. Vertical crazes in the hull near the root of the keel must not, however, be lightly dismissed as they are a sign that something is seriously amiss – and this something just might be a lack of reinforcement to the load-bearing components of the hull – ie the floors, mast support pillars or main bulkhead.

While gaining access to the internal hull of a wooden boat, unless the soles and linings have been irrevocably fixed with malice aforethought, is not too involved a procedure, the glassfibre interior modules to be found in the modern production yacht are a curse and seem specifically designed to defeat any thoughts of inspection of shipside or bilge space. If an otherwise smooth and unobstructed moulding has been fitted with access hatches it is not necessarily safe to assume that the cause of the query has been dealt with!

If there is a centreplate, check for movement along the lower edges of the case: look for flex cracks in a GRP boat, lavish application of sealant in a timber vessel. Bear in mind that pivot bolts do wear, even those made of stainless steel, and it is best to budget for regular replacement. This also holds true for lifting tackle of both centreplate and lifting keel. While there are few faults that cannot be put right by a judicious application of money, it is still best to know about these before a final commitment is made to purchase.

Rudders, in particular rudders constructed of glassfibre with encapsulated metal stocks, are a prime source of defects,

A trail sail outfit at its simplest – a single axle axle trailer, family saloon and four berth marine ply cruiser designed to weigh in at well under one ton. Remarkable stiffness combined with light weight can be achieved using modern resin glues.

defects which are inherent from the very outset and which may escape the notice of the keenest eye until actual break-down of the laminate occurs and the trailing edge splits apart. GRP skegs are inclined to flex, even a heavy section soundly fastened and bonded (which, in all too many instances, they are not). Skegs also are subjected to severe strain when a bilge-keeler on a drying mooring persistently makes a three-point landing, with much of the weight borne by the skeg. Whatever the cause, widespread crazing along the root is quite common: check for a 'bandage' of roving and resin or the give-away signs of filler and fresh paint! Neither is it unknown for a skeg to crack half-way down, often as the result of heavy or repeated grounding (if cracks here are spotted, the rudder and heel bearings must be considered suspect as well).

Fixed transom-hung rudders, also those which lift verti-cally, may also be injured by collision, grounding or even by snagging a mooring. Even where the blade appears sound, take a careful look at the transom gudgeons and pintles and, if there is crazing around these, budget for repairs (not forgetting the possible cost of cutting through the internal GRP cockpit moulding in order to gain access to bolts). Failure of the rudder offshore is a serious inconvenience, not to say an alarming one, but only in exceptional circumstances would it endanger the boat; given time and searoom, it is always possible to rig up some sort of jury steering. But let it happen in crowded waters – for example a summer Sunday at Lymington – and there would be hell to pay (to say nothing of the resultant insurance claims).

Check the inventory

Having examined the mast and assessed the method of raising and lowering it, the inventory (and this includes the sail wardrobe) should be weighed up: this is for the purposes of negotiations and an agreed insurance valuation of the vessel. If furling gear is fitted, there may only be one headsail, which should be provided with a sacrificial leech strip to guard against the effects of ultra-violet light upon the fabric. Just the same, if sailing in coastal waters, a storm jib and inner stay upon which to set it is an advantage and, for those bent on serious offshore cruising, so is a storm trisail – even though it may never have to be set. For gentler days a spinnaker or cruising chute can be relied upon to alleviate boredom!

Opinion is divided as to whether a small boat, one whose passages may be limited to the demands of a young crew, needs to be laden with electronic navigation aids. Common sense says probably not – manufacturers insist, yes. For what it's worth, my own thought is that instruments should be regarded as a confirmation of, rather than a substitute for, the basic principles of navigation. This viewpoint is unfashionable, but total reliance on electronics can instil a false sense of security, and a degree of self-reliance is essential on any vessel. Still, few would argue against fitting an echosounder and log. More important by far, though, for the cruising boat, is money spent on a first-rate compass, preferably one which can be adjusted. The siting is problematical on a small boat – obviously the card needs to be seen without neck-wrenching contortion on the part of the helmsman but it also needs to be clear of objects causing deviation – such as the inboard (or stowed outboard) electronics, including the autopilot, the VHF and – often overlooked – any cockpit loudspeakers! Cameras with built-in light meters can have a pretty drastic effect on a compass, too.

Adequate ground tackle is also a vital part of the inventory and one which receives too little consideration – presumably because the advertising brochure shots, focusing on sparkling seas, sun and sandy beaches, are intended to make sailors forget that the sea can be pretty intimidating at times – and that bringing up upon a sandy beach in a gale could smash the boat to splinters. Also there could be a time when the only thing standing between salvation or sinking will be the anchor and chain. It simply should not be taken for granted that a sheltered anchorage or marina berth can be reached in bad weather, but it does seem to be a pretty general assumption to judge from the frayed warps and toy anchors carried on some boats. This optimistic turn of mind usually also extends to the cleats and fairleads, many of which would simply fail if the boat ever had to ride out a storm at anchor.

Minor structural ailments or deficiencies in the inventory are not automatically reason enough to rule out a particular purchase, but every possible effort should be made to determine these from the start. Professional advice should draw attention to hull problems and recommend the appropriate treatment, but especially in a case where there is a degree of haggling about the final purchase price, it is important to have a clear understanding as to the extent of the inventory (and, if there is any hedging on the subject by vendor or agent, get it in writing). Without actually implying dishonesty, it does happen that a kedge anchor, barometer or other minor (but not inexpensive) items may go missing, a few fenders absent themselves, possibly a storm jib or spinnaker disappear from a locker. And who is to say what was in fact present in the first place. Most vendors, whether private or in the trade, are straightforward and pleasant to deal with but nothing should be taken for granted. And the old warning of *caveat emptor* holds as true when buying a boat as it does in any other transaction!

7 The Tow Vehicle

Accepting that the prosaic matter of personal finance may prove to be a decisive factor in the choice of a trailer sailer, the nature of the proposed tow car should not be ignored. Thoughts are bound to be drawn towards one of the currently fashionable muscular four-wheel drive vehicles but for most of us it is the family saloon or estate car which will be pressed into service.

Since vehicle design motivation has been aimed at increasing economy, the development of compact, relatively light cars whose engines are remarkably efficient for their cubic capacity, has been a growing area. Excellent all-rounders though these vehicles undoubtedly are, few models with an engine capacity of less than 1500 cc can reasonably be expected to tow anything heavier than a camping dinghy or dayboat, maximum length around 18 feet, without some signs of strain.

The maximum permissible weight of boat and trailer – for it is this combined figure which is taken into account when calculating the recommended upper payload limit – should ideally not exceed the kerb weight of the car; only a small degree of latitude should be tolerated. It is generally recommended that, for safe towing, the load should not actually exceed 90% of the vehicle's kerb weight, so it is this figure which must be kept in mind, even though at present the recommendations are not legally enforced. From a strictly practical point of view, however, the engine horsepower is arguably of at least equal importance, since a car gasping uphill in first gear, a backlog of frustrated motorists trailing in its wake, is not going to contribute greatly to safety on the road. In spite of the fact that trailing with a payload in excess of the figure recommended for the tow car does not appear to directly contravene the law (though it might conceivably, if proved, invalidate the car's insurance), legally the onus is on the driver of the vehicle to ensure the safety of the tow at all times and ascertain that it in no way endangers road users. A crawling car and trailer, inciting fury and frustrating all efforts to overtake might well incur the wrath of officialdom and a subsequent fine.

Theoretically, working out the maximum tow weight for the vehicle concerned is simplicity itself. The kerb weight (which must, when towing, be shown on the nearside of the car) will be given in the manufacturer's handbook, the kerb weight being the weight of the vehicle without occupants but with coolant, engine and gearbox oils, a full tank of fuel and such tools as would be normally carried – jack, wheelbrace etc. Generally that figure will be spot on, although there could be exceptions where individual cars have been customised, and some models are notably prone to this! Modified bodywork, or a transplanted up-rated engine may make a considerable difference to the handbook figure.

But the actual weight of either boat or trailer may equally be open to question. A trailer purchased new from a reputable firm can be pretty well guaranteed to conform exactly to the manufacturer's data sheet, but there is no such assurance with a trailer of unknown provenance or age. There are trailers a-plenty in existence which have been welded up to what could, at best, be described as 'agricultural' specifications without so much as a glance at the Motor Vehicles (Construction and Use) regulations or a word of professional advice. By the same token, many manufactured trailers have, over the years, been subjected to ad hoc 'improvements': in either case the unit could be far heavier than estimated. Quite apart from any physical considerations such as strength or suitability of the backbone or mechanical components, the weight must be established because of the mandatory legal braking requirements. These stipulate that if the designed axle weight exceeds 750 kg, or its laden weight amounts to half the kerb weight of the tow car (and there are few trailer sailer packages which would not), the trailer must be fitted with brakes. Unbraked trailers are only acceptable where the gross weight amounts to under half the car's kerb weight, which effectively rules out almost every boat with permament accommodation.

There is even more possibility of discrepancy between specified and true figures in the case of the trailing weight of the boat itself, even a boat hot from a state-of-the-art production line constructed to engineering tolerances, so take it for granted that, regardless of any figures quoted by designer or builder, the boat will be heavier (rarely will it be lighter unless stripped to the bones for racing). A slap-happy laminator making free with the resin might result in a 10% weight gain in a 22-foot glassfibre boat. A timber craft, especially one

which has been lovingly built by an amateur, regardless o
cost, could well have scantlings and joinery far in excess o
specifications. Wood is surprisingly heavy stuff, so allow for c
20% discrepancy. A journey to a public weighbridge will pu
paid to any argument, though if the boat has already beer
bought in good faith there will be an understandable tempta
tion to ignore information which may prove unwelcome
Hence the importance of allowing for a possible margin c
error.

It is worth pointing out that a normal cruising inventory
adds a fair bit to the vessel's deadweight: don't forget the
anchor(s) and chain, outboard and battery – to say nothing o
the ship's stores: canned foodstuffs, perhaps ten gallons o
fresh water (enough to last a family of four for two days), a
case of beer, a couple of bottles of medicinal spirits, books,
clothes and the general paraphernalia of everyday sailing
life – all these easily stack on another 200–300 lb. True, such
odds and ends can be loaded into the car rather than the
boat, but the same engine will still have to haul the lot!

The ideal vehicle

However, to return to the tow car (and for the purposes of this
book it is private cars other than commercial vehicles, for
which the legal requirements differ slightly, which are the
subject of discussion), there is no doubt that some vehicles are
better suited to towing than others by virtue not only of their
power to weight ratio but also because of ground clearance
and suspension. In all of these, estate cars score over saloons
or hatchbacks every time as they do on interior passenger
and luggage space. Accepting that purchasing a second car
solely for use in towing is probably out of the question, should
there be a case for replacing the day to day transport, it is
worth seeking out a car versatile enough to cope with the
needs of the family round town, long-legged enough for
relaxed motorway driving and which sips rather than slurps
fuel. There are vehicles combining these attributes yet
rugged enough to haul a ton or so of boat and trailer around
the countryside without undue effort, so avoiding the need for
route planning by contour map!

The currently popular four-wheel drive models are certainly tantalising: tough, powerful and designed very much
with the extrovert in mind. Most, of course, pass their entire

A line up of tow cars and yachts at the Friedrikshaffen Boat Show.

lifespan on the urban drag and never come within hailing distance of grouse moor or slipway for all their vaunted off-road capability! But this image enhancement comes with a high price tag attached. Admittedly, there are one or two exceptions such as the Dacia Duster and the sporty-looking but rather underpowered Suzuki Santana but these lack some refinements which might be regarded as desirable for everyday driving. Eventually, after five years or so the price, even of the more forceful vehicles, does drop to an affordable level but spares and routine maintenance can be quite costly and the larger four-wheel drive models are notoriously thirsty. This is reflected in the higher initial and re-sale prices of the more economical diesel versions.

Rumour has it that some four-wheel drive vehicles will overturn without warning given the slightest opportunity, but given that they do have a high centre of gravity when compared with a 'conventional' car, it would take extreme carelessness to achieve this in the normal course of events. Unlikely as it is that anyone engaged in towing a boat would be disposed to venture off-road from choice, the all-terrain capability is a major marketing angle, so much so that there have evolved a number of kit-built clones which look the part and may to some extent act it. Usually, ground clearance is, on close inspection, little higher than that of an ordinary car although the jacked-up suspension may suggest otherwise. However, even if a vehicle is able to take rough ground in its stride the loaded trailer probably cannot, so, unless there are other reasons to take off across country, this ability will be of little use.

Though there are not at present or in the foreseeable future any immutable rules governing the relationship of engine capacity to the trailed load, it follows that in order to eliminate undue stress – to driver, other road users and the engine itself – the more powerful the engine the better. On the debit side, the more cc's under the bonnet, the greater the fuel consumption – and also initial cost and running costs – though not necessarily the price second-hand. But for long-distance driving – perhaps down to the south of France or through the Pyrenees to northern Spain, there is no substitute for sheer horsepower. It will also be reassuring to know that the car has power in reserve to cope with an unexpectedly steep or treacherous launching site.

Diesel engines have been refined to the point where their major drawbacks – noise especially and less than spine-tingling acceleration at all speeds – can virtually be discounted. The economy and reliability of these power units have at last been recognised and good second-hand examples are quickly snapped up. It hardly needs pointing out, though, that no matter what the number, capacity and configuration of cylinders, it helps if they are firing as nature intended! And nothing short of coolant loss will bring an engine to an untimely halt as fast as an attempt at towing when piston rings, valves or bearings are worn or damaged.

Transmission – auto or manual?

Automatic transmission is now an optional extra on the majority of cars, even the smallest, but whether it is one which should be specified as a matter of course for a tow car is open to argument. In the end it boils down to personal preference and perhaps, experience. The torque converter of an automatic gearbox, providing as it does, maximum torque at low speeds, gives an ultra-low first gear, well suited to hill starts and equally happy pulling away with the payload of boat and trailer; it should just about eliminate any tendency to snatch at the tow hitch when pulling away and some drivers do claim that towing with an automatic is less stressful.

Others though, miss the psychological reassurance of being able to decide for themselves exactly when to change down into low gear and use the braking power of the engine to slow on bends or hills. Even though the torque converter does precisely this without human interference (indeed it may well anticipate the power requirements far more accurately than the majority of drivers) no-one committed to driving with a manual gearbox is likely to be easily convinced of this. Whatever the merits of the case, automatics do tend to return a slight but measurable increase in fuel consumption compared with manual cars.

Clearly, no-one would neglect to check oil and coolant levels of any car before setting off on a long trip, but it is especially important in the case of an automatic to check the hydraulic fluid in the gearbox as well. Since the engine will be subjected to extra strain when towing, it may run hotter and it is advisable to fit an oil cooler to prevent the oil thinning as its temperature rises. Engine tuning is also critical as is the tick-over speed; if this is too high, the vehicle will pull away from stationary in a series of violent jerks but, more to the point, the higher engine revs may also override the effect of the brakes, rather as though driving with full choke.

Nor is a manual gearbox free from possible ailments; worn syncromesh on lower gears can be actively dangerous if the driver relies upon the gears to assist braking. Missing a gear may cause loss of concentration and this, even if momentary, inevitably occurs at the least convenient moment. Linkages too can give trouble, though usually not without some prior warning – and in aged gearboxes, the lower gears can develop a nasty habit of jumping out. If this happens when the engine is under load, it is disconcerting and the loss of power could be critical: if it takes place on overrun, when the pressure is off the accelerator and the engine is acting to slow the car on a steep gradient, it will be actively hazardous.

All too often the 'weak link' of a manual gearbox is the clutch. This comes in for ferocious abuse when towing – and when launching or recovering a boat too, for that matter: the aroma of smouldering clutches is a piquant accompaniment to a summer Sunday on the slipway! Never, never hitch up for a journey if the clutch has started to slip; it can only get worse and even the lightest foot on the pedal won't save it.

Overdrive on third and top gears or, as is now more common, a fifth gear, can contribute to fuel economy on good roads even if on country lanes there will be precious little chance to make use of either facility. Some care is needed if cutting out the overdrive on a slippery road, as the action is instantaneous and can cause the driving wheels to skid.

Power steering, formerly an extra restricted mainly to large cars in the luxury bracket, is fast becoming 'de rigueur' on middle range models – and even on urban runabouts. It is not an extra for which I would myself lay out additional cash, but apart from disliking the absence of sensation in the steering at speed – also the tendency to oversteer – I have twice suffered the loss of the hydraulic fluid through a defective rack. Although not unheard of, this rarely happens suddenly and the increasing sluggishness of the steering is progressive, though with care the car may be driven until the fluid can be topped up. However, each time it happened to me with little prior indication, and in heavy traffic, and the resultant wrestling matches with the wheel are not amongst my happiest motoring memories. But to be fair, when power steering is good it is very good and it takes much of the sheer physical hard work out of winding the tow through congested traffic or serpentine country lanes. And if the car's normal use is in town or city, the increased ease in parking will come in very useful.

Brake failure is another driver's nightmare but fortunately one which is rare, as a sudden failure is almost always brought about by a fault in the hydraulic system. Regular inspection of all hoses, pipes and clips should prevent any trouble and, naturally, the fluid must be kept topped up as necessary. Since the brakes tend to come in for more work when towing there is a tendency to overheat and it is worth enquiring about modified linings which help counteract this. A servo unit makes lighter work of driving but it may take the driver a little while to grow accustomed to the feather light pedal pressure.

Springs and shockers

The suspension, even of a large and powerful vehicle, may not necessarily be well suited to towing. Although a sports car will have excellent and usually very firm suspension, the ground clearance will almost certainly be too low for comfort, and it will be lowered still further once the boat and trailer are hitched up. Modifications to the springs will be very expensive if indeed possible. I towed for several years with a

The twenty foot Pioneer, trailable by a large family car.

three-litre MGC whose power was never in question – but whose exhaust system generally had to be retrieved in sections from the slipway after launching the boat!

Up-rated shock absorbers are readily available and, although primarily aimed at the caravan market, these are just as suitable for trailer sailers. Adjustable shockers, which give a hard or softer ride to order are another alternative: certainly not a cheap one but highly effective and frequently fitted to competition cars. The adjustment is simple enough, little more than a turn of the screwdriver – but not everyone would fight for the honour of carrying out the task once the car has the inevitable winter accumulation of grime and mud! Helper springs are a third alternative; these are relatively simple to fit and remove much of the compression which effectively converts the standard spring into a solid unit, one which having lost its resilience, will give the passengers a hard time of it, detract from road-holding ability and possibly even result in damage to the vehicle. These helper springs, by the way, only come into effect once the increased loading is applied; they do not alter the normal handling characteristics nor do they hoist the rear end off the road like a street rod!

Less expensive, but still quite functional, are air springs: spheres of plastic filled with air under high pressure. If used in conjunction with leaf springs, these are simply clamped to the upper edges and absorb a good part of the shocks encountered when towing. With coil springs, two air springs are inserted within the coils. In either case, manufacturers claim a fitting time of only ten minutes and, since there are no moving parts, there is no wear or maintenance.

Self-levelling suspension, where fitted, is a real asset – invaluable to those whose sense of adventure seduces them from motorways and on to the dubious surfaces of country roads (French country roads being especially noted for uneven pavé, unlit roadworks and unexpected excavations).

Towbars

Many new cars are fitted with a towbar and electrics as a matter of course but the provision of a unit is neither unduly difficult or prohibitively expensive (though if buying a second-hand car, with an eye on the budget, it will pay to search out a car with lighting socket and towbar already in position). If acquiring a new towbar it should conform to British and international standards and ideally should come from either the vehicle manufacturer or a reputable specialist company. The tow ball for European countries has for some years been standardised at 50 mm for the majority of trailers up to a 3500 kg capacity; an older car might still be fitted with one of different size but it is usually simple enough to fit the standard model to the existing towbar.

The towbar itself is a simple enough piece of equipment, a transverse bar attached by side arms to the chassis or sub-frame, or with the use of special stiffening panels, to the floor of the boot. But especially in the case of a vehicle past its first youth, it is vital to ensure that the structure is sufficiently sound to withstand the stresses imposed upon the fitting, and the annual MOT is not a guarantee of this. Quite a few cars are designed so water is trapped in odd corners of the boot and below the petrol tank where, just like wet rot in a timber boat, it carries on its depredations unseen.

Assuming the soundness of the car, the fitting of the towbar should be within the capabilities of those with reasonable mechanical aptitude – although professional advice is advisable. The electrics and lighting socket might be another story and tapping into the circuit of a modern car with its sophisticated and complicated systems is not a job for the inexperienced. Older cars as a rule do have simpler wiring but over the years modifications may well have been made and it is very doubtful if the loom will bear much resemblance to the wiring diagram in the handbook.

Although the 7 pin '12N' socket is generally fitted for trailer towing, it might pay to fit the double variant, the so-called '12S' (S for supplementary), if the boat's lighting is to be operated from the car battery when cruising overland. Since the majority of boats will have their own electrical supply this facility will not be strictly necessary, but a split charge relay incorporating a blocking diode (to prevent accidental discharge of either the car or boat battery in the event of a malfunction) will be worthwhile.

8 The Trailer

However well-suited the car may be to its job of hauling boat and trailer across country, the configuration of the trailer will have a marked effect upon the ease with which this is accomplished. The design will, in addition, play a part in the stability of the outfit once on the road and also affect the launching and recovery of the boat. If there can be said to be a drawback to towing a well-balanced payload safely within the recommended weight limit for the car, it is simply that the driver may entirely forget that there is 20 feet or so of glassfibre and steel following placidly astern! Comparatively few of the thousands of people who cheerfully trundle all manner of contraptions around the country, not only boats and caravans but horseboxes, van trailers and even snack bars, ever give a thought to the chassis and mechanical components of the trailers, trusting, usually quite rightly, to the manufacturer's specification and quality control.

But a boat trailer should be regarded as quite a specialised piece of equipment for it has, after all, a multi-purpose role. Not only must it transport the boat (which will in most cases be heavier than a caravan offering a similar number of berths) but it must also support the hull and this, once out of its natural element, is in many respects a fragile object. Bear in mind also that the boat will, in all probability, be over-wintered ashore on the trailer as well. And in order to facilitate the launch and recovery the trailer must be able to cope with a wide range of gradients and surfaces; even with today's commercialisation and the wholesale concreting of much of the coastline, there still exist more crowded and potholed assault courses than gentle tarmacked slopes undiscovered by other boat owners!

Support for the hull

Support of the yacht while trailing is absolutely critical; not even a purpose designed trailer sailer will be immune to the stresses of a cross-country journey. These stresses constantly shift slightly according to the road surface and camber and there will be occasions when they may be imposed upon a section of the hull least suited to dealing with them. Some yachts are simpler to support in safety than others; boats with a long shallow centreline keel or ballast stub distribute the loading equally over a larger area than would a deep fin-keeler although, of course, chocks or rollers must be carefully sited in order to keep the boat upright.

Bilge-keelers present few problems: the loading of the keels is taken by the internal stringers, or moulded stiffening in the case of a GRP boat, and once on the trailer, the keels or plates can be quickly secured in twin channels; apart from restraining arms port and starboard on the trailer the bilge-keeler needs little support other than chocks under bows and stern. A high performance yacht with a deep and narrow fin must, on the other hand, have a number of supports to the underside of the hull with particular attention paid to the area immediately fore and aft of the keel itself. Bilge support will be needed too and this should, for preference, be aligned with strong points in the hull such as structural bulkheads.

Best of all, naturally, is a custom-built cradle which distributes all strains evenly. These strains, by the way, could well be greater than might be supposed if the yacht is being lived in when over-landing: aside from the stores essential for a fortnight's cruise, four adult crew members will add around six hundred pounds of weight – highly mobile weight, thoughtlessly distributed at that! Since the stores and crew may total half the actual weight of the yacht it is easy to see just how easily the hull or fittings could suffer structural damage if the trailer, cradle or supports are not precisely tailored to it.

Except for the smallest and lightest yachts, those perhaps with camping or overnight accommodation and for which a cradle can be home-constructed from glassfibre, a top-quality trailer, purpose built to give adequate support for a one-off design will be expensive; it may in fact account for (at a rough estimate) somewhere between 10 and 15% of the price of a new boat. Trailers specifically built for class and one-design boats might, due to the number built, work out slightly cheaper – but only slightly. Cost cutting though is not really the best policy ... the boat's life expectancy may be at stake! Unfortunately there is not only a financial premium exacted for a good trailer, the more suited it is for long distance trailing (and incidentally long term storage) the heavier it is likely to be, in spite of the fact that the stability and roadholding on

A Leisure 17 bilge keeler showing easy alignment of a bilge keeled boat on its trailer – though supports and rollers would be added to the trailer prior to trailing and launching.

tow will be superior. As a rough guide, the simplest trailer for a 17-foot boat will probably weigh at least 135 kg, for a 19-footer, in the region of 210 kg and for a 22-footer around 380 kg, twin axle and slip cradle versions being proportionately heavier. The overall length of the trailer must not exceed 7 m, unless it has at least four wheels and is towed by a goods vehicle weighing more than 3500 kg, in which case an overall length of 12 m is permitted.

In its simplest form a boat trailer consists of a single backbone or A-frame fitted with a tow hitch. A cross-member carries stub axles, wheels and suspension unit. As mentioned previously, once the combined weight of trailer and boat exceeds 750 kg, the trailer must be fitted with brakes including an inertia device, intended to pull the trailer up should it become detached from the tow car. There must also be a parking brake. The trailer must also be provided with lights, indicators and reflectors in accordance with current regulations. Except for a light, easily manhandled dinghy trailer there will also have to be a jockey wheel fitted for manoeuvring once the trailer is detached from the car. In most cases a ratchet winch will also be needed to assist in hauling the boat back on to the trailer after sailing.

Trailer configuration

Trailer types can basically be divided into three: the simplest single-axle unit, and the break-back and swivel-beam types. Each of these may have single or twin axles and can be modified to accept a flat-bed cradle, though this will have to be craned off the trailer itself. A fixed or break-back trailer can also be designed to accommodate a slip cradle – a cradle with its own set of wheels which slide down channels once the trailer is tilted to the necessary angle, for the launch or retrieval of the boat. There are also tilting trailers, rarely encountered in this country, which pivot the boat horizontally around its axis for trailing in countries where width restrictions demand it. In practice a width restriction of 2.9 m for load and trailer combined (the width of the trailer alone when towed by an ordinary car should not exceed 2.3 m) does mean that any hull whose beam to length ratio approximates to the norm would fall well within the limits of the average car. Since the maximum tow length for car and trailer combined is 18 m only, those at the wheel of certain American nostalgia mobiles of the 50s should have reason to be concerned!

Not only do varying trailer configurations affect the handling characteristics under tow, they make quite a difference when launching, too. Although, given an acceptable loading, a single-axle trailer is perfectly roadworthy, if regular long-distance driving is on the cards, it is logical to invest in a twin-axle close-coupled four wheel trailer. Undeniably, it will be both heavier and dearer, and it may even lower the average speed of a journey, but on the grounds of increased safety alone, it is worth it. With the smaller diameter wheels which can be used with a twin-axle trailer, the centre of gravity will be lower and in consequence, roadholding much improved. Then too, the marginally longer wheelbase will help to damp out pitching in the fore and aft plane though this may only be noticeable at speeds over 40 miles an hour or so. Admittedly, there will be two pairs of wheel bearings to grease instead of just one and the tyres, being smaller, run hotter; these factors, though, are a small price to pay for the reassurance that, should a blow-out occur, the trailer is not going to whip smartly round out of con-

trol and take charge of the car, a hazard not to be lightly dismissed when towing. Though it is hardly a recommended procedure since it would almost certainly write off the tyre
involved, it is quite feasible to drive on (slowly) with one flat
tyre if this cannot be changed at once. One other advantage of
a twin-axle trailer is that it makes it possible to launch in shallower water, though against this must be set the lower ground
clearances of the smaller wheels and the fact that, once the
trailer is unhitched from the tow car, it is heavy to haul around.
(Any loaded trailer should be manhandled with circumspec-
tion – quite apart from the risk of crew members pulling mus-
cles or otherwise incapacitating themselves, it is not unheard
of for a tyre to be wrenched completely off the wheel rim).

The break-back trailer on the whole, is best suited to smaller
trailer sailers. This type, as the name suggests, hinges at a
point about one third of the way aft from the tow hitch and this
section, once tilted, forms a steep slope down which the boat
slides easily. It should be possible to launch the boat without
total immersion either of wheel bearings or crew. Usually,
though, a bit of strenuous exertion is needed, particularly on
recovery, so as to bring the craft far enough forward on to the
trailer for the backbone to snap back into place. Just so long as
there are enough rollers (all of which turn freely) and a powerful winch to haul the boat up the steeply inclined portion of the
trailer at the end of the day, a break-back trailer makes light
work of both launch and recovery. However, the sharp angle
adopted once the trailer back is broken can make it easy to
miscalculate the depth of water and a careful eye must be kept
on any transom mounted outboard; even the lower edge of the
transom itself may be subjected to abrasion or damage from
coming into unexpected contact with the surface of the slip.

The swivel-beam trailer, usually with fixed backbone, has a
pivoting cross-member found fitted with numerous heavy
rollers which serve to locate and steady the bows of the boat as
it leaves – or on recovery meets up with – the trailer. With judicious assistance from the winch it makes light work of slipway
operations and is of great help controlling the boat in strong
winds and boisterous on-shore seas.

Slip cradles

A slip cradle, carried piggyback on the main frame of the
trailer, is arguably the quickest and safest method of

launching; the wheeled cradle supports the boat during transport, also at the critical moment when it enters the water, and the cradle arms go a long way towards protecting the hull topsides from being damaged by adjacent walls or other craft in the vicinity. Whether the trailer is of rigid or break-back type the launch procedure is similar, except that with the rigid model immersion of the trailer wheels will be unavoidable since otherwise there will not be depth enough for the boat to clear the cradle. There is an alternative where the slipway is steep enough: the trailer, guided by the crew, can be unhitched from the car and allowed to slide down towards the water, progress being checked as required by a winch mounted on a car's towbar. A break-back trailer would be more likely to be used in conjunction with a slip cradle and although the trailer winch will be needed to retrieve the boat, it should be quite possible to launch without topping seaboots. There are snags; it is not always as easy as suggested to guide the cradle wheels back into their channels on the parent trailer and for this reason, although these channels should only be slightly wider than the wheels, the ends need to have a slight outward splay. (The slip cradle wheels, by the way, must be large enough to avoid being snagged if winching over an uneven surface – yet not be of such dimensions that the yacht bounces around exuberantly when being trailed!)

Not surprisingly the slip cradle and trailer involves a high financial outlay although it is possible, given professional assistance or at the very least, advice, to modify a suitable heavy duty trailer. For those with a one-design, sailed by local clubs, who only occasionally trail, perhaps to a race meeting or the holiday cruise, co-ownership is a good idea: club members jointly purchase one or perhaps two parent trailers and each individual boat has its own slip cradle which can be used for storage ashore or simply be winched aboard the trailer when wanderlust makes itself felt. A wheeled cradle simplifies the task of positioning the boat on shore and this is much appreciated by boatyards (though I have noted that they don't seem to alter their pricing structure to take account of it!).

Buying second-hand

Whichever type of trailer is favoured, it must be borne in mind that, as with both the tow car and the yacht itself, it is subject to deterioration. When buying a second-hand trailer it is most important to ensure that it has been properly maintained: washed clear of salt water and road spray, all greasing points and wheel bearings packed. An air of neglect may mean that the asking price is low enough to be attractive but do be certain that defects or damage can be put right at reasonable cost: trailer repairs are not cheap, in fact you may find there are occasions when getting one roadworthy will involve more outlay than the purchase price of the actual boat.

Corrosion, not surprisingly, is about the worst single threat to the unit, not only to the chassis but also to all anchorages for bolts and moving parts. Neither is it always self-evident; indeed it can be all but impossible to detect once those time-honoured standbys, paint and filler, have effected a disguise. Judiciously employed, these can obscure just about any attack by what the motor trade refers to as the 'metal maggots' for a time, but only for a time. Take a tip from the car dealer's book and run a magnet over the frame – any effect on the vendor may be purely psychological but is sure to be worth watching! Once it has become widespread, corrosion is both difficult and expensive to deal with.

Although there are one or two bespoke trailers where stainless steel is a major structural component, the trailer backbone will generally be fabricated from ordinary rolled steel either of box section or a 'U' section channel; either, if not well protected, will be liable to rust, though when a section of channel is afflicted, this should at least be simple enough to spot. With a box section, the most serious corrosion will be likely to work insidiously from within unless all metal has been thoroughly inhibited and painted or, as it would be in a high quality trailer, galvanised. Although it is generally regarded as preferable to leave a box section open so that water can drain freely, occasionally the interior may be filled with oil and sealed.

Nothing will offer an absolute and indefinite guarantee against eventual rust although eternal vigilance will help forestall it; if and when external surface deterioration is visible in a box section, it may be too late for any economically viable remedial action; the trailer will be useless except for salvage or scrap. Minor bubbles and loose flakes of rust can be scaled off with a hammer and wire brush – and an initial investigation with a light hammer will, in most cases, reveal the true extent of any corrosion: an amalgam of metal, rust and filler produces a distinctive dull and flat tone sound

A twenty-four foot Strider class micro multihull on its custom trailer. From the dismantled hulls and bridgedeck to this state of readiness took two crew members forty minutes flat. Note the supports along the centreline of the trailer frame – these are for the cross beam stowage. Although bulky, the trailer can be quite light in construction since the cat only tips the scales at six hundred pounds all-up (ex ship's stores, that is!).

when tapped. Really extensive surface scale might necessitate the dismantling and grit blasting of the trailer; this is of course, perfectly all right if the underlying steel is basically sound, but the problem may be shown to be more serious than previously supposed and it would be best to discover this at the outset!

Once it has been established that the trailer in question is not corroded beyond the point of no return, an on-going programme of preventive maintenance will go a long way towards keeping it that way. Quite apart from traditional rust deterrent coatings (materials such as red oxide and other metal-based primers) there are on the market effective rust inhibitors such as Owatrol which bonds to light surface scale forming an impervious water resistant skin. External protective coatings such as cold galvanising paint or Hammerite will, if applied strictly in accordance with manufacturers' instructions, put a stop to depredation of the metal and also enhance the general external appearance of the trailer.

It should be noted that a generous application of anti-fouling (which, coincidentally, matches the underbody of whatever boat is perched on the trailer) does not offer much protection, except of course from marine flora and fauna, which are not liable to prove a major hazard unless the trailer is habitually parked under water! But it does suggest that the annual re-paint has been rather hurried! Hot dip galvanising is the best possible protection for steel and ensures the continued integrity of surface protection unless subjected to physical damage. If buying from new, galvanising well justifies the extra expenditure. It should also be thought about in the case of an older trailer which has been grit-blasted back to bare metal: added to the initial time and cost of dismantling and cleaning back the components, the extra spent on the galvanising should hardly be noticed and, especially in the long term, it will be money well spent.

Assuming the trailer is to be stripped down to essentials, the removal and examination of all through-fastenings and U-bolts would be carried out as a matter of course. Otherwise, however, these might escape detailed inspection, important as this is, since the U-bolts in particular are an essential linking part of the trailer's anatomy. A few years of accumulated paint can lend an illusion, spurious though it may be, of solid metal where none really exists.

Routine maintenance

While it is working for its living, a trailer will usually be the subject of some measure of care and attention but, come the end of the season, it is frequently just left to sit around, forlorn and neglected (though the boat may be covered, the engine winterised and the sails duly sent away for valeting!). If left without even the semblance of a winter overhaul, the trailer may suffer a marked degree of depredation which may not be realised until it takes to the road at the start of the season. Quite apart from the insidious action of any residual salt upon all metal parts, damage to the tyres can be expected if the weight of the trailer – even bereft of its boat – rests entirely upon them for months on end. Ideally the loading should be taken by blocks or axle stands but, even if this has been done, when checking the trailer over, do take a close look at the tyres since they are subject to the same legal requirements as the tyres of the tow vehicle. As with a car, radial and cross-ply tyres must never be mixed on the same axle.

The wheels must be inspected for signs of damage to rims or of cracks, and the number and condition of studs should also be noted. Even where a trailer has been professionally built, the wheels with which it left the factory may have been replaced for various reasons; if it has been amateur built, even where the main component parts were purchased from a specialist firm, it is a fairly safe bet, that in the interests of economy, the wheels came from a scrap yard and already had a few thousand miles on the clock! Whether or not the donor vehicle's type can be immediately established, a visit to a car breakers may be needed in order to acquire a matching spare – travelling without one is asking for trouble and expense, not to mention the risk of the boat and trailer becoming the focal point of an accident if temporarily abandoned by the roadside in the event of a puncture.

Suspect the condition of wheel bearings no matter how smart or how well presented the trailer. Severe wear will be apparent if the wheel is firmly grasped and rocked, top to bottom: there will be noticeable play, possibly accompanied by binding as the wheel is rotated. Once clear of the ground it should turn smoothly and silently. Inspection and re-packing of the bearings should be carried out as an essential preliminary to any journey but is all too often overlooked on the very first one – the delivery of the newly acquired boat!

The suspension of many a home-built trailer – and there might be a suspension unit fitted between wheels and trailer frame – might easily have the best part of a generation's road use to its credit; indeed, if leaf springs have been employed in the construction, this will almost certainly be the case. Modern manufacturers widely favour suspension units of tough and long-lasting rubber. Strong as leaf springs are, over the years they gradually lose their resilience and slump wearily to earth (so further reducing ground clearance which tends to be rather on the low side even when leaf springs are new and in their prime). Establish whether the leaves still have the designed curvature ie lowest in the centre and not the reverse! Ensure in addition that no leaves are broken: this is potentially dangerous and would without doubt be considered to be in breach of legal safety requirements. While inspecting the springs, take the opportunity to investigate the condition of the spring hangers too: these are noted areas for unsuspected corrosion and the weakened metal can endanger the structure of the trailer.

Brakes and other items

Brakes, when fitted to the trailer, must comply now with EEC directive 17/320 which states that coupling and properly matched brakes, together with appropriate linkage, must be fitted, as must a parking brake capable of holding the detached trailer on a gradient of 18 per cent – though it would be foolish not to carry chocks or wedges as an added safeguard when leaving the trailer. Trailer brakes have a hard time of it: even with the greatest care and the best designed units, contact with water is inevitable and so is the start of corrosion. The handbrake should always be released during the lay-up period to avoid problems when it is time for removal of the wheels and drums for inspection of the brake linings. If these are worn, it may mean replacement of the shoes in order to ensure even braking; brakes which snatch or operate unevenly place a strain on both driver and tow vehicle, and may also cause a corroded brake wire to snap. These wires and clips often prove to be in a precarious condition, often being totally overlooked in an otherwise meticulous programme of maintenance.

The brakes normally fitted will be operated by hydraulically damped overrun couplings; this type have, in fact, been mandatory on UK-built trailers constructed after October 1982. The brakes automatically come into action along with the brakes on the tow car and their effect is reassuringly obvious especially when descending steep slopes! Older trailer couplings are still fitted with a manual reversing catch where the driver has to get out and physically disconnect the braking system before attempting to back the car and trailer but an ever-increasing number now have an 'auto-reverse' catch as standard; this has been stipulated on all new trailers fitted with brakes and constructed since April 1989.

For those faced with building a trailer from scratch, or with a comprehensive repair and restoration project, it is the relatively complex coupling/tow hitch which will, on a braked trailer, account for the major part of the budget. Of necessity it is an expensive item, containing as it does the overrun mechanism, reversing catch and, of course, the tow hitch itself. Just as much the subject of corrosion as of wear, it should be regularly greased and the protective gaiter replaced if perished.

There are few things more frustrating than to find, after carefully going over both boat and trailer preparatory to a trip to the water, with trailer ready to be hitched up, passengers waiting impatiently for the off, that the wretched jockey wheel simply cannot be raised. This is one fitting where trouble-free operation is taken for granted, and it is yet another which somehow gets missed off the winter checklist. Usually penetrating oil, grease and ultimately muscle power will free it, but only after considerable delay. When inspecting a second-hand trailer, it will often be noticed that the jockey wheel has one or more flat sides. This is due to the boat having been towed along the slipway with the wheel locked in situ! Such a mishap is probably the second most frequent that occurs during launching or trailing. (The third is arguably that of omitting to secure the jockey wheel's retaining pin against vibration: the noise when the wheel makes unscheduled contact with the road surface as the car belts up a motorway will echo in your ears for a long time!)

Rollers also must move freely in line with the hull section or they may damage the underbody. The winch too needs regular greasing and should be tested prior to setting out. Though terylene webbing is often used, wire is still quite common; it comes under great tension and may also be subjected to snatch strains in excess of the designed loading. See that the wire cores are sound, even if there is slight surface rust, and that there are no 'soldiers' (broken wire strands which can cause rather unpleasant and painful cuts, very susceptible to infection).

Whilst in the process of checking the moving parts, make sure that they do so only as and when required: this particularly applies to slip cradles and the break-back mechanism.

Reflectors and lights, both the lenses and bulbs, must also be intact and functioning and this is doubly important when trailing on the Continent where you may be forbidden to proceed further if the light is defective – it must be put right immediately and on the spot. The lighting requirements for boat trailers have grown ever more complex but a list of requirements is given in the appendix at the end of this book.

Once the trailer is in first-class order, possibly loaded with the yacht (and stores for the holiday), it would be rather a shame to have everything stolen! But as any police officer (or insurance broker) will admit, this happens all the time – boats vanish from car parks while the owners take a quick break, from boat yards and even from gardens. One precaution against the opportunist thief is simply to remove a trailer wheel (take the spare as well, though, or the exercise is a waste of time). A coupling lock, highly visible, is also a good deterrent although possibly not if an intending thief has established the owner's movements over a period and is confident of sufficient time to actually cut through the backbone of the trailer and then haul the outfit away on a low-loader. It is not at all likely that such organised criminals would consider a small sailing boat worth their while – the market is after all somewhat limited, but with some of the more exotic and extremely expensive power craft, this has indeed been known to occur. Accepting that no anti-theft devices are absolutely infallible – though it would be very much in your own interest to ask your insurance company what they regard as good practice in this respect – the dreaded wheel clamp is as good as anything – even if it does smack of joining the enemy ranks!

9 On the Road

Before embarking on any long journey, it is recommended that the car be serviced – although there is also a body of opinion which is strongly in favour of having this carried out at least a week beforehand since hitherto dormant minor faults often seem to rise uneasily to the surface as a direct result.

Pre-travel preparation

Check all fluid and oil levels, also tyre pressures – not omitting those of the trailer. It is not a bad idea to have the car wheels balanced since imbalance causes vibration of the steering and undue wear of mechanical components. Almost certainly the headlight beams will be too high once the trailer lowers the rear of the car and, in any case, these will need adjustment for Continental driving.

The fan belt is a well-known trouble maker if it breaks; the pundits claim that a makeshift replacement can be fashioned within minutes from a stocking, but I for one would like to see them try it on a motorway hard shoulder, in darkness and rain with articulated lorries roaring past, only inches away! Wear is not at all difficult to see – nor is the tension hard to check before setting out. Hoses and clips are as important to a car as a boat, when in either case failure can result in near catastrophe.

Some spares should be carried, especially when driving abroad, and an emergency breakdown kit can be hired from the major motoring organisations: this includes those parts most likely to give trouble, such as points, spare fuses, hoses and clips. Additional items such as plastic tape, seizing wire and bulldog wire grips are as useful on the car as they are necessary on the boat. Don't forget that not all car jacks will be capable of lifting the combined weight of boat and trailer (and the majority of car jacks can only be used in conjunction with the specific jacking points on the car). A hydraulic bottle or trolley jack is best (although some of the cheaper trolley jacks have only a very short lift) and it is also a wise precau-

Fig 6

Car and trailer checkpoints

1   Ensure headlamp beams are not too high: once the boat and trailer are hitched up the weight will tend to lower the rear of the car and tilt the headlights skywards.

2   See that you have good all-round visibility; wing mirrors are essential, in Britain as well as when driving on the Continent. In some cases an extension mirror fitted over the standard wing mirror may be useful – so too may be a small stick-on 'blind spot' convex mirror. If towing a deep-draft keelboat (which may resemble a miniature apartment block once loaded onto the trailer) consider also the kind of periscope mirror commonly used by caravan owners.

3   It is usually best to transport a rigid dinghy on the roofrack – making certain that it cannot be skewered by the mast if the spar shifts! Bulky items can be lashed underneath the boat. There is now on the market at least one dinghy which doubles as a stowage box – or vice versa depending upon priorities.

4   It helps if the boot lid or hatch back can still be lifted once the dinghy is in place.

5   Bear in mind that the jack designed for the car may not be strong enough to lift the combined weight of trailer and boat – and may in any case call for a different jacking point.

6   Have a good look at the car's ground clearance once the trailer and payload are attached. Common victims of rough road surfaces are the exhaust, back axle and, if the springs of the tow vehicle are weak, possibly even the engine sump.

7   Ensure that a safety chain or wire strop is attached between towbar and trailer.

tion to carry chocks or axle stands to take the weight off the jack while the wheel is changed. Most probably the car's wheel brace will not fit the nuts on the trailer wheels and a spider type, which accepts four different sizes may be the

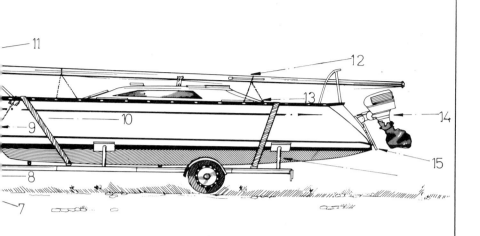

Double check the security of the jockey wheel: it should be held in place by a pin or bolt; if not, vibration will loosen it and cause it to descend abruptly en route.

Bows should be lashed firmly into place against the pitching encountered on the trailer: place blocks of foam rubber or similar as an anti-chafe precaution under all ropes. Terylene webbing, tightened with ratchet buckles, is an excellent method of securing the load.

It is best to lash the mast so that the projection is over the bows rather than the stern – just ensure you lash it well so that it cannot impale any load carried on the roofrack! If intending to camp onboard whilst overlanding, try to arrange matters so the hatches can still be opened but a separate lashing for the hatch is vital when underway.

Tape the spreaders to the mast along with standing and running rigging – but remember to untape them *before* stepping the mast!

If the stanchions splay outboard of the deck – and they very well might if the deck is cambered – remove them before taking to the road.

The outboard is best carried below (for security reasons as much for any other) but if carried on the transom the propeller must be protected and covered by an orange bag.

Boarding ladders, like jockey wheels, are prone to making unannounced descents – see that the ladder is secured in place.

Check that the supports are aligned with the hull and that the boat is properly supported along its length.

answer. The extra leverage is worth having, too. Aerosols which both effect a temporary puncture repair and also re-inflate the tyre are a great idea; many are the encouraging tales of salvation by spray can! Unfortunately they best work on tubeless tyres and only then if the puncture is fairly minor so I don't put too much faith in them. That said, there can be no harm in carrying one – there are circumstances in which it might allow the car and trailer to drive clear of a potentially risky roadside situation.

At lunchtime stops it is advisable to glance at oil and coolant levels and also check the temperature of the wheels. Should these seem unduly hot to the touch, it might be an early warning of bearing seizure. Constantly watching and listening for signs of this can lead to a form of paranoia: whilst driving down the Autoroute du Soleil, heading for the holiday port of La Grande Motte, the often anticipated squeak became ominously audible. Resigned, I stopped, checked the wheels. Nothing, the metal was cool. As soon as I was back on course the noise resumed in all its intensity. Another summary halt, another investigation; as before, nothing. This pantomime was repeated over and over until realisation dawned: the sound was simply that of crickets shrilling along the roadside. As I stopped, so they stopped, alarmed by the intrusion. Once the car was in motion, it posed no threat and the sounds of French insect life carried on with undiminished fervour.

When towing, there should always be a safety linkage between trailer and car – with a braked trailer this must be incorporated into the braking system as an infallible precaution against car or trailer opting to go it alone! Given the efficiency of modern tow hitches this eventuality can be all but discounted (though there is always the human factor to contend with!). Less unusual is for the boat to shift position on the trailer and there have been plenty of instances where boat and trailer have indeed parted company as a result of careless lashing on; sometimes the ties are conspicuous by their virtual absence. It is by no means unusual to see trailed boats bowling along connected to the trailer by a nose rope alone. But, apart from this head rope, there should be at least two secure ties across the boat as well as two diagonally placed to prevent any possibility of fore and aft movement. Heavy duty terylene webbing is excellent as it does not chafe and, if used in conjunction with ratchet buckles, can be secured quickly and without fuss. When using rope, care must be taken to place fabric or foam rubber pads under areas which might be subjected to chafe – both to protect the hull and the rope itself. Partially encasing it with hose is quite effective.

Where the deck of the boat is heavily cambered, as many

are, the stanchions will have an outward splay and must be removed for trailing. (Although it is accepted practice to fit stanchions in this manner, they are an absolute menace to any boat berthed alongside in harbour – but that's another matter!) Assuming the boat is to be lived aboard when on the trailer, it must be possible to open the main hatch for access and the forehatch for ventilation. This means that the mast has to be secured so as to leave both hatches clear and purpose-made chocks or supports may be needed. Never use the standing rigging of the mast to keep it in place and, should it be necessary to use any rope halyards, check them thoroughly for any chafe before sailing.

In the case of a Bermudian sloop rig, the spar will be rather longer than the boat itself. It is best for the major part of the overhang to be over the bows where it can be secured on to a suitable support post – but see that it cannot possibly foul any load which may be carried on the car roofrack! There is a permitted rear overhang of one metre if the projection is clearly and visibly marked by a red or orange bag (or streamer). With a projection of between 2 to 3.5 m there must be a triangular striped end marker board fitted. If the load overhangs more than 3.5 m, complications ensue: side markers are needed, there must be a driver's 'mate' – and police must be informed in advance.

If the outboard is carried on the stern (though not the ideal place for it in the case of a light sailing boat) the propeller and any projecting parts must be covered and prevented from causing injury by a protective high visibility bag. Admittedly, whilst this might avoid damage to any pedestrian heedlessly ambling into the stationary outboard, it could hardly be considered to offer much in the way of protection in the event of even a minor traffic accident but it is, nevertheless, a legal requirement, and non-compliance could lead to prosecution.

Never underestimate the effect of vibration upon all ties and lashings: if anything can possibly shift, then it will do so – though generally (unless a rope actually carries away) most movement will take place within the first twenty minutes of a journey simply because the webbing or rope will stretch, albeit slightly. It does, therefore, make sense to examine the load shortly after setting off and before encountering motorway conditions.

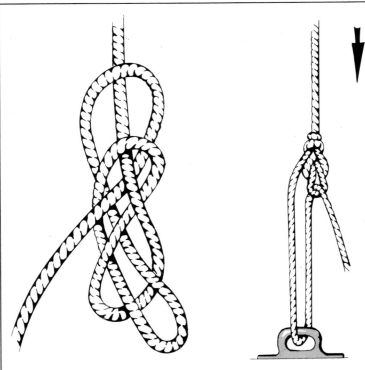

Fig 7
This knot, a bowline on a bight (occasionally referred to as a trucker's hitch or dogging knot) is useful when it comes to tensioning rope lashings. It can also be used to set up lifelines, standing rigging – even to tighten a kicking strap.

Towing technique

Travelling with the yacht hitched up astern is by no means the daunting matter it might appear. A boat is less lively under tow than a caravan since it is blessed with a better aerodynamic shape and has considerably less wind resistance. With a lower centre of gravity it is also more stable.

The keynote of a relaxed journey is forward planning. This should eliminate the worries about impossibly steep hills, long, rutted country lanes which have no turning and rush hour urban traffic. The motoring organisations are very helpful as regards advance route planning and it helps to keep an ear open for traffic information on local radio stations, so have a list of frequencies to hand. On the journey, the driver should be free to concentrate on handling the car and mastering the technique of driving with the tow. And here it is smoothness that counts above all. Avoid sharp gear changes, try to avoid slamming on the brakes on the verge of road junctions – and don't attempt any high speed cornering! It may be stating the obvious but the driving should be defensive rather than aggressive, and try not to inconvenience others. Precise road positioning assumes a greater importance when towing since the trailer effectively lengthens a car's wheelbase; corners should be taken slightly wide to avoid clipping the kerb. More dangerous than kerbing – and an even greater risk where the yacht overhangs the trailer by several feet – is that if the turn is misjudged, the playload may swing out sharply into the adjacent traffic lane and hit another vehicle. Changing lanes abruptly is ruled out if in heavy traffic so noticing – even anticipating – roundabouts and filter lanes can save unwanted excursions up one-way streets or time wasted turning the car round for another try!

If you have never before driven with a tow or are out of practice and doubtful about your ability, hitch up the trailer (preferably unladen) and get in a couple of hours' driving early in the morning on a road with little traffic or better still, an open space where you can learn to judge the turning circle and attempt reversing without fear of hooted objections.

Of all manoeuvres, reversing is the trickiest (and some of us never become truly adept at it) but it really only calls for slow and precise steering. It is all too easy to over-correct and so a close watch must be kept on the trailer's trajectory in relation to the car. Start off with car and trailer in line with each other, wheels straight (if the reversing catch is not automatic, operate it now or the brakes will lock on the moment the car moves backwards). Double check that there are no obstacles such as letter-boxes or litter bins too close for comfort – and that no-one has parked a bicycle or pushchair below the driver's line of vision. Assuming such hidden dangers are absent, start to reverse and – slowly – apply opposite wheel lock to the intended direction of turn. At this point it is critical not to put on too much lock too fast for the trailer could jack-knife – and there are times when the only method of extricating it from this embarrassing state of affairs is to unhitch and wrestle it into re-alignment! Once everything is lined up and pointing in the desired direction, straighten the wheel, disengage the reversing catch if necessary and move off – keeping a wary eye open for vehicles or pedestrians who may have moved up unnoticed in the meantime.

Unimpeded all-round vision is vital whether driving in town, country or motorway. Depending upon the height and beam of the yacht, it is often helpful, if not legally mandatory, to fit extended wing mirrors – and there are times when a periscopic mirror could also be an asset. The law insists only that any vehicle registered after January 1978 must have an exterior offside mirror when towing and, if the interior mirror does not facilitate a clear view behind, also a nearside mirror (this would be an absolute necessity when towing on the Continent in any case). Mirrors fitted to the front wings must be spring mounted. A couple of times over the years, I have been stopped by a police patrol and an officer who took over the driving seat with the sole object of peering through all mirrors. It is a good idea to carry along a spare piece of mirror glass and a roll of plastic tape. I once drove nearly two thousand miles through Spain and France to return to England eventually with boat, trailer and car unmarked and intact, until both wing mirrors were wrenched off – courtesy of vandals at Plymouth docks.

As a rule, even during rush hours, drivers of heavy vehicles are fairly considerate to those towing (and often downright wary into the bargain since they realise that the driver might only hitch up two or three times a year). The same, regrettably, cannot be said of all car drivers and there are those upon whom the car and trailer acts as does the proverbial red rag to a bull! But pedal and motor cyclists – particularly the radio-controlled couriers – are especially dangerous. They move faster than anticipated, have the habit of sneaking – or flashing – past on the blind side where they are invisible except at the very last moment. In stationary traffic too, pedal cyclists have the unnerving tendency to steady themselves against the trailer and, on clear roads, racing cyclists are prone to slipstreaming, tucking in so closely behind the boat that they just cannot be seen. Needless to say, this is pretty foolhardy as their brakes are not likely to stop them in time if the vehicle behind which they are hitching a lift is forced to pull up suddenly.

But, even after a driver has gained considerable experience towing and grown accustomed to the wiles of other road users, stationary objects may, by the mere fact of their existence, turn out to be peril enough! For example, it is far simpler to proceed blithely into a petrol station than it is to leave without assaulting flower pots and tangling with pipes, airlines and other associated fripperies encountered on forecourts everywhere. Nor is the destruction of overhead fitments and signs unheard of; true, a flush-decked lift-keeler on a close-coupled four-wheeled trailer may not cause undue worry in this respect but a 22 ft bilge-keeled boat, drawing three feet and perched upon a twin-wheeled trailer may top 9 ft from tyre to tabernacle – this I know to my cost as does one attendant who persistently waved me on to a garage fore-court in Guildford! But garage canopies apart, there are also plenty of overhead rural hazards: overhanging branches frequently come in for a bit of unscheduled pruning.

Winding country lanes place a premium upon the driver's skill with gear changing in a car with manual transmission; once more the watchword is smoothness – a snappy down-shift may bring about a skid while the selection of a high gear at too low a speed will place a strain upon transmission and engine. In the case of an automatic vehicle the lowest forward drive should be selected but it is wise to consult the manufacturer's handbook for advice specific to each individual make and model.

Snaking and pitching

After being subjected to the delights of the so-called urban cycle, motorway driving should come as a blessed relief. But the open road may also be an excuse to open up the throttle and speed may creep upwards without the driver's being aware of it. High speed, though, is one of the contributory causes of snaking, one of the least pleasant dramas associated with any trailed payload. The term is an accurate description for the behaviour of the trailer: it starts to swing from side to side with increasing momentum and, in an extreme case, the tail, so to speak, wags the dog. Alarming as it is for the driver (and passengers) of the tow car, it also jeopardises the safety of any overtaking vehicle.

Twin axle trailers are less liable to snake than the single axle type, but given adverse road camber, uneven tyre pressures (or a puncture) it can take place with any trailer, any-where. Caution should be exercised when driving in gusty conditions or exposed situations but the undulation can be initiated by nothing more than the slipstream of a passing juggernaut. No matter what, resist the temptation to stamp on the brake pedal for this will only make matters worse; speed must be lost gradually and the vehicle handled as delicately as though caught up in a skid. This, naturally, is much easier said than done and it takes cool nerves to remain in control when in the middle lane of a motorway, overtaking perhaps, and being overtaken in turn. With a well-designed, correctly loaded trailer, snaking is held to be a fairly rare occurrence; unfortunately it isn't and this is borne out by the number of damping devices of which the aptly named 'Snakecharmer' stabiliser is arguably the best known.

Pitching is uncomfortable for the passengers rather than directly harmful to the trailer or car – but anyone at all susceptible to motion sickness would find the pronounced seesawing of the car's rear end just about intolerable. At worst it just might overstrain the vehicle's rear suspension (and indeed it may be a weakness in springs or shockers which exacerbates the problem in the first place). Often, though, the blame for the unsettling motion is the direct result of poor loading, with either too much or too little nose weight upon the coupling (recommended nose weights for cars are always laid down in the handbook; usually a figure of 36 kgs seems about right for a boat weighing one ton). Too much nose weight is as bad as too little and some attention should be paid to aligning the boat correctly on the trailer and to stowing heavy items; treat the boat on the trailer as though it were at sea: ensure that, whenever possible, excess weight is kept out of bows and stern and try to stow the heaviest items low down. No matter how much care is expended on balancing the yacht and stores, however, there will inevitably be an additional loading imposed on the rear suspension of the car so, bearing this in mind, be aware of any sounds suggestive of the exhaust, engine sump (or in certain cars, the master cylinder) making intimate contact with terra firma. Occasionally the towbar itself may be too high and the fitting of a drop plate should help – at least it will prevent any possibility of the trailer wheels lifting from the ground under way.

At the launch site

On arrival at a launching site, in particular one which is new to you, take your time – no matter how enticing the prospect of getting afloat is bound to be! (Should you have miscalculated your timing it may, regrettably, be impossible to do other than take your time: public slipways in popular areas tend to be overcrowded in summer, even more at the approach of high water.) Walk down to the water's edge, take note of the direction of flow – and its strength – even if you have already ascertained the time of high water from the tide table. Judge the force of the wind and the point from which it is blowing in order to establish the course which must be sailed once the boat is launched. Whilst engaged on reconnaissance duties, see whether there are any potholes, ruts or areas of mud that the car and trailer might find it impossible to negotiate. If the slipway is narrow, mark the edges with a couple of canes, these will be invaluable for lining up the car when reversing since it is not hard to actually back off the edge of the slipway – with consequences that can easily be imagined.

Raising the mast

With a small boat whose mast can be stepped easily by one or two people, it is often simplest to carry out this operation whilst the boat is still settled firmly upon the trailer; it may in fact prove difficult to do otherwise if there is any weight to the wind. It seems too obvious to mention but do ensure beforehand that there are no overhead power lines between boat and water! The first task, though, would nearly always be that of setting up the stanchions and lifelines since this frees the deck of clutter and gives the crew a sense of security when moving around.

   Much now depends upon the actual method of raising the mast. With the new generation of trailer sailer a good deal of thought has gone into the simplification of the process – completely justified in view of the long, light (and very expensive) spars upon which are set today's high performance, high aspect ratio rigs. Up to a point, it is the length of the mast rather than its deadweight which determines just how awkward it will be to raise or lower. This is because of a tendency to twist sideways, often to the point where it can sway out of control and overpower the crew. Many smaller yachts step the mast on nothing more substantial than an adjustable heelplate with provision for a pivot bolt, which is adequate for, say, an aluminium mast of up to 22 ft in length, assuming the section to be proportionate to the length. With only a slight increase in overall dimensions, however, some form of preventer will be needed to keep the mast in line whilst it is being raised or lowered, and a large number of cruising yachts rely upon a tabernacle which does this to some extent.

A tabernacle is generally provided with two bolts, the lower being withdrawn before moving the mast which is then left free to pivot on the upper one. In some instances there is only a single through-bolt, so wedges need to be inserted under the heel once the mast is vertical, but this is rather a hit-and-miss method only suitable for the smallest craft with lightly stressed rigs).

Raising a spar stepped within a tabernacle is simple enough: the heel should be placed between the two uprights and the topmost bolt should be fastened into place, though not over-tightened. The foresail or spinnaker halyard – whichever is closest to the mast truck – should be taken forward to the stemhead and rove either through the stemhead fitting (assuming this is provided with a roller) or through a block made fast to a strong point in the eyes of the boat. Never, never attempt to take the weight of the mast by a direct pull to hand (especially if the halyard is of wire). The shrouds can be left in place, as can standing backstays and runners, though the former may need to be eased off before raising or lowering.

At this point the normal drill is for one crew member to haul away while the second takes up position well aft, first to support the mast at shoulder height, then as it rises, to walk forward gradually with it. If the stern of the boat sways, put chocks beneath it, for good balance is important. As the mast approaches the vertical, ensure that the bottlescrews have not capsized themselves on to the chainplates for this will stop the mast being raised the last few inches (a short length of large diameter plastic pipe slipped over the rigging screw and toggle should stop this from happening). With the mast safely upright and now balanced, the hand aft moves forward and attaches the forestay. If the mast was stepped single-handed, the physical act of making it fast can be very awkward. It helps to use a wire strop slightly longer than the rigging screw with a carbine hook on the lower end: have one end ready shackled to the forestay just above the bottle-screw and simply snap the hook on the forestay fitting if there is room or to a split pin through the stemhead roller. This eliminates any struggling to make ends meet and does away with any likelihood of the mast unbalancing and crashing to the ground! (The same technique can also be employed where headsail furling gear is fitted, of course.)

Boats in which mast raising (and lowering) is a daily rather

Fig 8

i An 'A-frame' seen from the front and side. Quite often the frame is curved so as to conform exactly to the deck plan of the boat. In all cases it is rather an encumbrance on the foredeck as it obstructs footwork and will make it difficult, if not impossible, to use the anchor locker where one is fitted. On a larger boat though, it is possible to secure the frame firmly and so utilise it as an extra foredeck grabrail.

ii The frame (A) should be rigged with a purchase taken to the stemhead and forestay made fast by a snap shackle or carbine hook to an eyebolt on its upper surface, the preventers (B) set up along with the cap shrouds (C). The mast is then ready for raising. There are several minor variants of this – sometimes the fore tackle is led through blocks on the frame direct to the stemhead, and frequently a check shroud (D) is made fast to the lower end of the frame. Both (B) and (D) can be tightened by a crew member with the aid of a simple jamming block on the purchase.

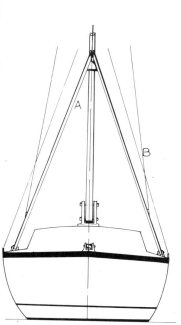

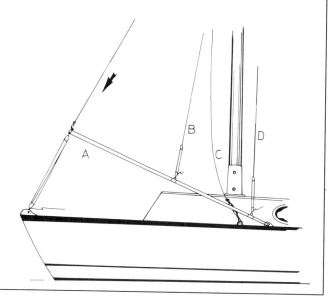

than a weekly occurrence – such as those based on the Broads or intending to navigate the Dutch waterways – tend to favour an 'A-frame' system. This eliminates sideways movement almost entirely and, with a yacht up to about 25 ft in length it should be possible, if necessary, to manage the mast single-handed. Effective as this method is, it does occupy a fair bit of space on deck – and, in the case of a craft with a foredeck anchor locker, the frame has to be partially lifted in order to gain access to the ground tackle – admittedly not much of a nuisance for inland waters where mooring alongside to a bollard or rond anchors is the usual practice but very impractical for cruising in tidal waters – where the anchor might be needed in a hurry. One variation on the 'A-frame' uses a purpose-built hinged pulpit, extending aft almost to the lower shrouds; it works well enough but the fitting looks a bit cumbersome on a small boat.

A temporary frame is rigged easily enough using the main and spinnaker booms. Secure the heels to deck eyes, chainplates or the pierced alloy toerail if fitted. Next, fasten a strop

Fig 9 Raising a mast with a strut. Often the spinnaker boom is designed to be used for this purpose, and special fitting is incorporated for its attachment just above the mast heel. This works well with a short or light mast, but a longer spar will not only tend to twist slightly as it comes upright, but may need an extra long strut (though if all else fails rigging a long line and taking it a good distance away from the boat before the hauling begins should achieve the desired objective in the end!).

Fig 10
Increasing the height of the winch may make it easier to control a mast whilst it is being raised or lowered – but make certain it does not foul the pulpit.

around the mast just above the spreaders to the apex of these sheerlegs then rig a purchase from there to the stemhead; this will control the mast quite effectively. At a pinch, either the main or spinnaker boom can be pressed into service alone but it must be set with preventer guys or there will be too much twist for safety. Many Dutch small craft (and a few in this country) have a slot set into the forward edge of the mast into which is inserted a strut with a block at the outer end; this serves the same purpose but is rather more rigid – nevertheless, when coping with a heavy or unwieldy mast, preventers will still be helpful if not actually essential.

Mast lowering is, on the whole, a much quicker experience. Everything is repeated, but in reverse order and assisted greatly by experience!

Although there are exceptions – such as the very light spars of the smaller Freedom rigs, if the mast is keel stepped it will be necessary to use a crane to lower it into place (unless there happens to be a convenient bridge, high quayside or large vessel nearby). Once the spar is in situ, though, it will be supported by the deck allowing the rigging to be set up in your own good time.

Time, regrettably, may all too often be of the essence. In summer, awareness of the number of yachts waiting their turn to use the slip or the boatyard crane may pressure you into overlooking small but unimportant details when raising the mast. Details, which if overlooked can bring great embarrassment (or worse), such as untaping the halyards, freeing masthead snarl-ups and inspecting all rigging links, clevis

Always, as a matter of priority, check over all rigging links, shackles and clevis pins before raising the mast. Otherwise . . .

and split pins. That this can also happen to professionals was demonstrated at a recent Southampton Boat Show where the exhibitor of a 30 ft sloop, no doubt hassled by the crane driver intent upon a tea break, not only clean forgot to set up the spreaders but also left the halyards taped neatly in place above the hounds – thereby making it impossible to send anyone up the mast to put matters right! Since the crane and driver then apparently vanished from the face of the earth, the vessel in question sported a somewhat unusual rig for the duration of the show.

Launch and recovery

It is one thing to write glibly about the delights of trailing, launching and recovering the yacht but the reality can, from time to time, be somewhat different. Getting it right is a matter of practice and this should be gained initially on slipways which have been checked out beforehand and which, for preference, are not too crowded: with a backlog of trailed boats and a falling tide, tempers quickly reach breaking point. It's pretty rare for things to go wrong with the trailer itself but rollers, the slip cradle or the jockey wheel can jam and sometimes the break-back mechanism can require a combination of brute force and heartfelt prayer. It should never be forgotten that the boat and trailer combination is heavy and if it is allowed to get out of control, it can cause injury to people or damage to cars and other boats. The most common disaster is for the trailer to slip off the edge of the slipway, shedding (and usually damaging) the boat in the process; I have also witnessed collisions between boats and reversing cars, and also watched in disbelief as a trailer sailer's mast was lowered (accidentally and with a resounding clatter) on to the roof of an adjacent vehicle. If this sounds alarmist, perhaps it should be pointed out that far and away the most common mishap is simply that of launching the trailer with the lighting board still in place on the transom!

The simplest method, of launching by immersion, is straightforward enough: head for the chosen slipway, then reverse down towards the water until the boat obligingly floats off. Or the tide comes in and lifts it off. Or – and it does happen – the process is hastened by the driver backing neatly off the edge of the slipway! So long as the trailer is well provided with rollers, launching at least is easy enough; recovery will entail assistance from a winch mounted either on the trailer or on the towbar of the car. This method ensures that at least one crew member suffers from wet feet, but it is the trailer which is prone to suffer most. Damage to wheel bearings is an all too common occurrence and its usual cause – discounting poor maintenance – is immersion launching. During the drive, the hubs become heated only to be cooled abruptly on contact with water. This contracts the air inside, forming a vacuum which sucks water in through the rear seal. Grit and dirt are drawn in with the water and these, together with the corrosive action of seawater, will lead to failure of the bearings very rapidly. It is possible to fit bearing protectors with sealing rings, but even so, the trailer wheels should be allowed to cool for half an hour or so before launching.

Before launching, make certain that the keel (or plate) and rudder are raised to their fullest extent and secured in place – the outboard, too, if it is on the stern for the launch. If there is an inboard auxiliary, see that there is nothing which can damage the propeller or foul it once the engine is started. It is best to plan ahead and launch on a rising tide: in fact, there is very little alternative if the boat draws more than three feet or so as otherwise the operation will involve the swamping of the tow vehicle! In the case of a light fin-keeler on a steep

High summer at Hamble: launching a twenty foot Timpenny from a break back trailer – the picture shows it just at the point where it starts to tilt sharply back.

incline, the boat can virtually launch itself or at least, with the trailer's jockey wheel lowered, slide down the slipway with only token exertion on the part of the crew. Indeed, preventing it from doing just that may be the main difficulty: a winch mounted on the car's tow bracket will be needed to control it, or rig a purchase around a tree or bollard (don't put your faith in lampposts – they are not, regrettably, as deeply rooted as they look). When using a car-mounted winch, never trust to the handbrake alone; place chocks under the wheels and have the wheels turned full lock as an added precaution.

Floating the boat clear of a break-back trailer follows the same general procedure. The trailer may need a bit of encouragement to 'break' but the weight of a crew standing on the rear section should provide this. Be careful to keep well clear of the join which can hinge more abruptly than expected. A slip cradle, too, tends to benefit from a bit of assistance on its way, initially at least. Once it does start to move, the weight should be taken on the trailer winch wire, paid out slowly – stand clear to one side just in case it does part, unlikely though this is.

Now the trailer is broken fully, the boat slides down the sharp incline and in the water – without the crew getting their feet wet.

Preoccupied by the serious business of manoeuvring the boat into the water, it's all too easy to forget to keep a firm grasp of the painter; once the boat is afloat, especially with keel and rudder raised, it can disappear down wind – or down tide for that matter – at an astonishing rate of knots! Whilst on the subject of lines, one word of warning: if the trailer has been uncoupled from the car in the anticipation of the rising tide lifting the boat clear, bear in mind that the trailer is a heavy object and will moreover, be in deep water, so keep a check line on that too. And it is best if all the available muscle power does not gleefully leap on board to move the boat away from the slip leaving a junior member of the crew to haul the trailer back up the slipway unaided – he or she may not be able to.

Recovery of boat and trailer usually requires a little more physical effort since everything must, of necessity, be hauled back up an incline.

Often all those concerned will be tired at the end of a day's sailing and tiredness leads to lapses of concentration and mistakes – it is best, if it can be arranged, to get a good night's sleep beforehand – or if daysailing, to try to arrive with enough time in hand to allow for queues at the recovery site, flat tyres – and lost car keys: all the little things which, together, make a memorable trip!

A slip cradle, unless well designed and engineered, may prove tricky to recover, at any rate until a bit of practical experience has been acquired. Locating the vessel precisely in the cradle is the first problem, one which can be partly overcome by painting reference marks on both boat and cradle. Once the boat is safely secured, there follows the task of aligning the cradle into the channels on the parent trailer, where again painted reference marks do help. There should also be guide arms on the trailer. Larger channels and wheels make matters that much simpler too (but remember that whilst pneumatic tyres give an easier ride on the way up on to the trailer, their buoyancy (combined with that of the hull) may cause the load to float away before it can be lashed in place!

Although there will almost certainly be a winch fitted to the trailer, this is a time when a second portable one which can be temporarily attached to the towbar will prove to be a blessing. With the extra purchase of this, backed up by the

Immersion launching a Cornish Shrimper on a twin axle trailer. Although the four wheel configuration does reduce the depth needed for launching, the Range Rover is still going to have his rear wheels under – unless he uncouples and allows the tide to finish the launch operation!

technique of hauling and sliding first one wheel and then the next, surprisingly steep slopes and dubious road surfaces can, in an emergency, be negotiated. In the worst case, it will be very useful in freeing the car if it gets bogged down (assuming that there is a handy tree or similar strong point).

One of the objectives of a dedicated trailer sailer is that boat, trailer and car become a self-reliant entity: able to launch, rig and recover the boat without outside assistance, no matter where, no matter what. But there may come a time when there is little option but to launch (or be brought out) by a boat lift or dockside crane. If venturing off the beaten track, it could pay to take along your own lifting slings – so far I have never needed them but have heard that some crane operators do expect them to be provided. No matter that the slings may be positioned carefully where the boat is stiffened by the internal bulkheads, do make sure that spreaders are used in conjunction with the slings to prevent compression stress upon the hull. The risk is greatest admittedly with a timber yacht of traditional construction but a light glassfibre boat can also suffer.

As said, advance planning counts for much, not only of the time schedule, the launching site and facilities and of course, the actual cruising waters, but also of the on-board inventory. Even allowing for the restricted space on a trailer sailer there are items of equipment which can improve lifestyle whether the boat is afloat or on the trailer, and it is these which form the subject of the next section of this book.

10 Living on Board

Accepting that the crew may be living on the boat while it is on the trailer – perhaps for two or three days at a time – their most pressing need will arguably be a light, sturdy and above all, rigid boarding ladder. Even with the small lift-keeler, the distance from ground to gunwale level is not going to be much under five feet and it could well be considerably more in the case of a bilge-keeled boat or one with an external ballast stub. True, most people would experience little difficulty in scrambling up from the trailer, but not on a regular basis and, if burdened with shopping or small children, the whole thing can turn into something approaching a commando exercise. Lightweight nylon or rope ladders require a knack to negotiate and if used, the lower end must be made fast to prevent it from swinging under the hull. If a permanent boarding ladder fitted to the transom is used, or if clambering over the stern at all, make certain there are supports under the hull to prevent it tipping.

Tents and overboom covers

Though no-one would seriously contend that living on board a small yacht is exactly a luxurious existence, while it is parked ashore and on its trailer there is, on the face of it, even less to recommend it. Due to the height of the accommodation from the ground, there is not even the option, available to caravanners, of extending the accommodation by means of an awning – duplex tents not yet having been invented. Some form of tent cover, though, is a distinct asset as it gives a degree of privacy for washing, changing and the preparation if not the cooking of meals. Privacy, as anyone camping shoreside on a boat will soon realise, is very much at a premium due to roaming groups of interested and speculative sightseers.

An overboom cover is the usual answer but, to be much use, there must be a minimum height of 5 ft between the boom and cockpit sole – no problem when the boat is rigged but not unfortunately the case with the mast lowered for trailing. So another means must be found to raise the boom and provide acceptable headroom. The aft end can be supported in a gallows fitted to the pushpit (or rudder pintles if there is a transom-hung rudder) but many boats today have booms so short that they do not reach as far aft as that. If this is the case, it is possible to make up a light support frame of steel tubing, inserted either in the handle socket of a top-action winch or in the stanchion base sockets. Where winches are fitted on the coachroof to port and starboard of the main hatchway, these can be used to take forward supports or alternatively, a second set of stanchion sockets can be pressed into service.

The cover can be made from PVC (which is stiff and hard on the fingernails in cold weather), canvas, light cotton duck or nylon – the latter two materials being easy to handle but inclined to translucency in certain conditions! If intending to cruise regularly in warmer climates, it is sensible to provide a flap on each side of the cover, which can be rolled back (kept in place by a strip of Velcro) to take advantage of any cooling breezes. (Equally, it is sensible to sew a strip of mosquito netting into place under it!) In any case, with a PVC cover which does not breathe, a ventilation flap should be incorporated to help avoid excess condensation on the inside.

Some trailer sailers, the E-boat being one, favour the fitting of an over-size folding spray hood which not only offers shelter when sailing (though the sheer size and windage are a bit daunting) but offers extra headroom below. This it does after removal of the main hatch and its garage (an operation which only takes a couple of minutes), the rear flap then being attached with press studs to the aft edge of the bridge deck: add on a larger flap and hooped support and there is the basis for quite a sophisticated cockpit tent as well.

A major contribution to privacy can be made by cockpit dodgers, which can be usefully supplied with pockets for winch handles, books (as well as sandy beach shoes!). These give protection against the elements when at sea too, of course – that is the main point of fitting them, but in the smaller yacht the windage is disproportionate and, in heavy going, they have been claimed to detract markedly from windward ability. When used in conjunction with a light awning (rather than a fitted tent cover which has to be tailored specifically to the boat and is, in consequence, quite an expensive item), these will make an appreciable difference to the standard of living on board.

In northern climes, most effort is devoted to the avoidance

of mist, drizzle and rain. But the sun can be hostile too and there are times when the shade provided by an awning comes as a blessed relief. Colours most restful to the eye are green and blue – though pessimists argue strongly for blaze orange pointing out that, in the event of an emergency, the cover can be spread out and lashed on deck, making the boat more easily spotted by the rescue services. Orange does, however, fade fast – reassurance presumably fading along with it!

Comfort in the cockpit

Those who sail can more or less be divided into two camps: the sybarites, and the stoics for whom everything is sent as a trial to be endured. And to these hardy souls, the very idea of upholstered seating in the cockpit would be anathema. In fact, it pays dividends to have cushions since an uncomfortable crew is unlikely to be an efficient one, and the crew can become most uncomfortable with their collective backsides parked for any length of time on slatted wood, GRP (in particular GRP with a moulded non-slip surface or, arguably worst of all, Treadmaster!) No matter what the covering of the cushions below decks, those in the cockpit should be of PVC as, besides getting wet, they will be thoroughly oiled with sun tan preparations (for this reason, don't leave them in place whilst sailing).

With boats built in almost every other country except Britain, there is fitted, as standard, a socket in the cockpit sole which allows the setting up of either the saloon table or a smaller, purpose-made one, perhaps with a weather resistant Melamine or GRP top. Why it is so uncommon here remains a mystery. Even in a cockpit which is too small to take a full-size table, it is possible with a little ingenuity to construct one which is at least big enough to act as a serving space and, if well fiddled or provided with appropriately sized holes cut through it, to keep vulnerable items such as bottles and glasses secure.

In a boat where the mainsheet track bridges the cockpit, a sheet of plywood can be cut to fit athwart the well, locating on to the track by means of a pair of parallel timber battens, hinge-down supports keeping it firmly in position. So long as the length is restricted to around 2 ft, it will not impede leg room too much but will still remain large enough to help relieve the congestion of crockery inevitably accompanying *al fresco* meals. Another method of creating a little more horizontal space is simply to slot a small tray/table by means of a tongue into a grab handle on a washboard and further steady this with a hinged leg – the space beneath on the bridge deck can still be used too. Individual trays can be made (or bought) which simply slot into a top-action winch handle socket (assuming that the socket is not already being used to support an over-boom cover). Both of these fitments are quite stable in use yet light and no trouble to stow when not needed, though it would be as well to ascertain the dimensions of the intended stowage locker before finally deciding upon the size of the table.

Light on the subject

Some form of exterior lighting is desirable, if not absolutely essential; many recently-built yachts are provided with a 12-volt lighting socket in the cockpit and clearly an electric light is much safer than a portable gas or paraffin unit which could conceivably start a fire if allowed to come into contact with the fabric of awning or cover. A lamp on a wandering lead, crocodile clipped directly to the battery terminals is a handy alternative – so, for that matter is a hand lantern or powerful torch (rechargeable from mains or by way of the car's cigarette lighter socket).

Small boat electrics are in the main regarded with a degree of ambivalence; often quite complex lighting and navigation systems rely solely on a single 12-volt battery which cannot be recharged by the outboard auxiliary. Things are different where there is an inboard engine with dynamo or alternator or if the outboard has electrics and a rectifier. Otherwise the comforts of home may turn out to be short-lived – high expectations flattening out along with the battery! But a heavy duty car battery will, if husbanded carefully, at least run domestic and navigation lights for the best part of a season of normal cruising although powerful navigation lights have a high drain and deck floods even more so.

To some extent a trailer sailer is fortunate in that a spare battery can be carried and charged en route by the car's alternator. It is frequently possible, too, to charge from the facilities of a marina or boatyard or in a mid-season crisis, should there be no other option, from a portable generator, hired at modest cost. Needless to say, both main battery and spare should be sited in a vented box and properly secured against all possible cavortings of the boat. The standards laid down for electrical installations are quite comprehensive and none but the most basic installation should be carried out without professional advice, or careful consultation of an up-to-date book on the subject. Indeed, so complicated has the specification become that there has been a small but notice-able defection back to the use of alcohol and paraffin as fuel for cooking and lighting.

Below decks

Well fitted-out though the cockpit may be, it is doubtful whether the crew will ever compete for the privilege of doss-ing down there, though opinions might undergo a sea change – in the Mediterranean, for instance. Much of the day-to-day domestic cycle takes place below decks and, with a full complement of souls on board, there are times when life will be hot, cramped, noisy and – dare it be said – at times somewhat malodorous!

The Red Fox has an outboard offset to starboard to allow full and free movement of the rudder. The vertically lifting rudder is simple and well engineered.

Once under way and sailing in fine weather, naturally, all discontent is blown away on the breeze, but given a long and frustrating grind to windward, an enforced stay in a hostile commercial harbour or worse, a couple of days storm bound at anchor, unable even to get ashore for a stretch, tempers start to fray. Life then becomes a matter of seeking comfort in the essentials of good food and undisturbed sleep. And these, of course, are the hardest things to come by.

Any functional limitations of the layout itself will soon be apparent but there may be little that can be done about those. But effects of poor interior design can at least be mitigated by well-chosen domestic equipment for this will undoubtedly help keep morale up; select top quality hollow fibre pillows (as opposed to lumpy cushions or damp sweaters stuffed with other sweaters) and light, soft sleeping bags, or duvets. If berths are unyielding and mattresses clammy, a backpackers' foam sleeping mat underneath acts as both insulation and shock absorber! And, if sleeping – or trying to – at sea, remember, lee-cloths are essential.

But it is in the galley and its utensils that the greatest improvements can be wrought for the least outlay. It is astonishing just what can be cooked on a simple two-burner cooker, even when the boat is doing its best to prevent it – and even more astonishing is the way in which food will be wolfed down, given a day or two for the crew to become acclimatised to the vessel's motion.

Galley gear

A seagoing cooker should be mounted parallel with the yacht's centreline and be gimballed so as to be self-levelling; the top must be fiddled too and ideally this rail should be adjustable. But no stove can operate at peak efficiency without cookware of an acceptable standard. The selection of the ship's pots and pans tends to be neglected with a motley collection of discards from home tending to predominate. While there is no call to splash out and acquire a set of colour co-ordinate enamelled cast-iron designer showpieces, high quality pans with well insulated handles really are worth their weight and stowage room and, moreover, are the safest in use.

Cast iron 'au naturel' was briefly fashionable but although

it heats evenly, it is ruled out for on-board use since the pans need 'seasoning' with hot fat prior to use and must be cleaned immediately after cooking and oiled again before stowage. And even then, in a damp atmosphere, some oxidisation may occur overnight. Stainless steel of a medium to heavy gauge is probably best overall (lighter grades overheat and carbonise their contents should the cook's attention be relaxed even momentarily!). Enamelled iron runs stainless steel a close second – smart and easy to clean, until the enamel is chipped, when the pan must be condemned. Nonstick pans are fine so long as they remain non-stick which, as a rule, they don't for long.

One of the most useful aids to cooking is a single tier steamer; a double one is unstable on a gimballed cooker. Steamed vegetables cook rapidly yet retain flavour and texture marvellously; fish and shellfish are excellent cooked this way too, so long as they are perfectly fresh, as also are good lean cuts of meat, and meatballs. All of these can simply be steamed over a herb stock which provides a good basis for a later soup or stew. You could also consider a pressure cooker though I have never succeeded with one myself. Nowadays there is little risk of inadvertently causing one to blow up but the size makes it difficult to fit into any locker. Besides, the quality and variety of modern convenience foods, which simply require heating, do really make taking a pressure cooker aboard superfluous.

But if some variants of saucepan can be more trouble than they are worth aboard – and I include amongst these such esoterica as dry-cook pans, woks (which won't fit on a fiddled cooker top) and iron griddle plates – there are types which are actively dangerous when cooking on a yacht. Resist all temptation to buy a set of aluminium camping saucepans with detachable handles: true, they are light in weight and easy to stow since they nest within one another but the handles are never rigid and heat up like branding irons. There is also a breed of frying pan still available (to my surprise) which is divided into three partitions, the cooker flame is channelled through the hollowed casting of the underside to emerge with the force of a blow torch (or rather three blow torches) and a nasty burn is easily inflicted. Chip pans, handy for large quantities of stew, are best confined to that purpose alone – quantities of super-heated fat really are a menace in any confined space let alone one constantly in a state of motion!

Ashore, the services of an electric kettle are very much taken for granted and, although some products are more user-friendly than others, the main criterion is that the element functions. But the boat's kettle, used on the stove top, really must be well manufactured, stable, with a heatproof handle and a narrow spout which pours accurately. Those whistling ones with wide spouts and an irritating cap which needs both hands to remove are worse than useless. And the incessant racket until they are silenced can ruin concentration at a critical moment – possibly more of a risk than that of the wretched thing boiling dry.

Any length is worth going to if it avoids the risk of burns or scalds, for these are acutely painful and incapacitating injuries, which are difficult to treat properly at sea, and susceptible to infection. One fact of shipboard life is that cooked food is often most appreciated when the going is arduous so, in consequence, meals or even hot drinks are a challenge to prepare. The wearing of heavy waterproof trousers may

Two's company, four, it has to be admitted, is a bit of a crowd – but then this lift keel Mirador is only eighteen feet overall. Note that the outboard is too close to the rudder to allow much angle of helm under way.

sound an unconventional precaution for the cook to take but it does provide some degree of protection against spilled food or boiling liquids (and being waterproof, they can be sponged clean if necessary).

Fire precautions obviously must be taken: apart from an extinguisher (to hand and in date), there must always be a fire blanket sited in the galley space. This is most effective in dealing with localised flare-ups, the sort which do tend to break out in the galley, but make sure that all crew members are instructed in its use: the first instinct when confronted with a blaze is to back away, but a fire blanket has to be thrown over it from close quarters.

Crockery and glassware is entirely a matter of personal preference. Plastic derivatives, even the best, eventually get scratched, discoloured – or suffer melt-down after being inadvertently left on a hot stove. Glass and china simply get broken – and slivers undiscovered during the clearing-up remain to menace the unwary (not to mention their potential for blocking the sink or even the bilge pump). It's a good idea to keep a few unbreakable mugs and disposable plastic glasses, just for use in bad weather or on night watches – where things are liable to be trodden on in the surrounding darkness.

Food storage

For storing cooked and raw food, a selection of polythene bowls with well fitting lids is needed. Aluminium cartons designed for freezer use come in handy too as food tends to sweat less in them. They also do sterling service as rough weather feeding troughs too – though don't attempt to eat anything piping hot from them!

Provisioning is a matter of personal choice – one governed both by the sailing area and the means, if any, of keeping perishable food cool.

A fridge is a luxury. Not one which is entirely out of the question, but one which depends very much on priorities. Finding a space is not necessarily the major problem – DIY kits are available and a small cold box can be tailored to fit into the most awkward corner. It is powering the compressor which is the chief difficulty; the battery consumption is very heavy indeed and is out of question for the majority of craft in the smaller size range. Bottled gas is a possibility but could entail the carriage of a relatively large bottle with the all the attendant pipework to current standards. Some earlier gas fridges also will not function safely with the boat heeled. Also, all refrigerators do, of course, need adequate ventilation.

It is questionable whether a fridge is worth the trouble. Capacity and ice-making ability will be limited and, once opened and the interior temperature raised, it will need a lot of energy ie fuel to re-chill the contents (and this is, to an extent self-defeating as the harder the fridge works, the more it raises the external temperature of its surroundings). One alternative, cheaper but, it has to be said, less effective is to carry a portable cold box, which can be charged by the car (only recommended when the engine is actually running, which gives an idea of the power consumption). Such a box will at least ensure a day or two's supply of the produce of the country until replenishments are to hand.

Many GRP yachts do have a cold box moulded in, but even when half-filled with ice, it can only be expected to keep food fresh for two to three days in a hot summer. Neither is it a simple matter to buy ice, even in fishing ports where there seems to be an abundance of the stuff. If the source of the ice is at all dubious (and, unless it has been acquired, poly-packed, from a supermarket it should be regarded as highly dubious) put it in the fridge in a lidded box or sealed bag and avoid letting it come into contact with fresh fruit or salads. Don't for heaven's sake stick a lump in the pre-prandial Martini! There has been great concern over food poisoning in recent times and the bacteria which are largely responsible can thrive on board. And one of the most welcoming breeding grounds for anaerobic bacteria – which flourish only in airless surroundings and bring about decay in double time – is in a closely lidded icebox. So do not leave anything to chance: once the last of the ice has melted, consume all food at once.

The simplest method of fresh food storage is to use a cool box or bag: bags might be best on board as they fold up for storage or squash down comfortably to make additional cockpit backrests!

Take the barbecue!

Having picked out all domestic gear with a wary eye on weight and stowability, chuck commonsense to the winds and take along a barbecue! If intending to cook ashore only, a small cast-iron Hibachi type is perfect, lighting easily, thanks to the large side vents, and cooking fast as the heat is well distributed. An Hibachi is, unfortunately, quite weighty and even more impossible to clean than the lighter tray types. For those who have everything there are beautiful 'barbies' engineered in stainless steel: these clamp on to the pushpit and are intended for festive meals when at anchor. One flip of the locking handle and all the unwanted by-products of the feast – the hot ash, spent charcoal, etc. can discreetly be jettisoned – just make sure that neither your inflatable dinghy, nor that of a neighbour, is in the line of fire! But with any 'conventional' type, charcoal and firelighters have to be taken along and these take up more than their fair share of locker space. All things considered, a better bet might be to buy a pack of disposable aluminium barbecue trays, pre-fuelled and quick to light. Certainly fresh-caught mackerel or swordfish grilled in the open over a bed of herbs is incomparable and is a holiday memory to be savoured.

But ... food is so much a matter of personal choice that any advice really requires a book devoted wholly to it. There is, though, much in the old saying that God sends the grub and the devil sends the cook!

Don't blame the cook ...

But, devilish as the goings-on in the galley may be, it would be unfair to assume automatically that any illness of the crew is the direct result of the chef's machinations. Seasickness is a very real problem and can lay low even the most fit and active people – and that includes a good many who claim never to have succumbed previously. Arguments are still rife as to the precise cause, though the symptoms are thought to be brought about directly by confusion in the vestibular apparatus – the body's built-in sensors of motion, angle and gravitational forces. Which is absolutely no consolation to anyone going through the first stage – that of being afraid they will die – or the second: that of being afraid they won't! An attack is unpredictable, some folk can cheerfully endure a force 6 thrash to windward without a qualm only to be found hanging miserably over the side when the boat is in a quiet creek, moving gently to her anchor.

At its worst seasickness reduces the human body to a pitiful state and the incessant vomiting is very debilitating. If the sufferer can be kept warm and there is room in the cockpit, fresh air is probably the best environment unless it is very rough, for nervousness appears to play a large part in the disorder. Certainly, he or she should be persuaded to take some liquid as bringing up bile from an empty stomach is exhausting; milk or drinking chocolate may be acceptable, cream soups too are sometimes welcome so long as they are not salty for this will exacerbate the thirst brought on by the vomiting. Tinned fruit is often palatable – preferably the least acidic types such as pears, apricots and peaches which are high in carbohydrate and easily digested.

There are many remedies, some of which work, some of the time and for some people. The drug cinnarizine, marketed as Stugeron, can be very effective but needs to be taken some hours beforehand and can induce drowsiness, as do the anti-histamine variants, such as Dramamine, which can help many sufferers. Bands which apply gentle pressure on the Nei-kuan point just inside the wrist are also claimed to reduce vomiting. So is hypnosis – and at £25 for a half-hour session it jolly well should! Other sovereign recipes include chewing dry bread, drinking an infusion of ginger root, also iced champagne – although the thoughts of a yacht owner watching Roederer Cristal being recycled into the spindrift would surely be too awful to contemplate!

Horrible as seasickness is, both for the sufferer – and the rest of the crew, come to that, it is not in itself life-threatening. But there is always a risk that acute food-poisoning could be mistaken for it (on the other hand, I have known one of the crew so wracked by cramps that it was believed he was in the throes of a heart attack and medical assistance was about to be summoned). Although it smacks of over-reaction, it could be justifiably argued that all watchkeepers should be fed differing meals – just in case.

The first-aid kit

Medical emergencies are, fortunately, not everyday occur-rences on board though a first-aid kit should, of course, be carried. The most usual mishaps are cuts, scalds, also bruises and fingers caught in deck fittings. All of these are unpleas-ant enough but can usually be treated without professional help. As well as the usual pain killers, antiseptic salves and seasickness preventatives, there should be a bottle of sterilising cleanser and wipes as well as medicine for stomach upsets (doubly upsetting in the confines of a boat). A good supply of lint and bandage should be carried along with waterproof adhesive bandage and small butterfly plasters which can hold quite long and deep cuts closed. Keep a couple of clean white towels for medical use too – also a hot water bottle which can be used to ease stomach cramps. Foreign bodies in the eye are a matter for real concern and can be tricky to remove; it may be risky even to attempt this if the boat is moving violently. Copious washing with warm mild saline solution does ease pain and may wash the object free; a fine (unused) artist's watercolour brush of squirrel hair or soft nylon, with castor oil, may be also helpful for extracting any grit which has lodged underneath the lid but don't try using this on the eye itself as it could scratch the cornea.

If cruising for any length of time, possibly in areas where there will be no recourse to outside assistance in the event of a medical complaint arising, your own doctor or the Port Medical Officer can prescribe a more comprehensive list of medicaments which can then be obtained from a pharmacist; this is on the understanding that all unused drugs will be handed back at the completion of the voyage. In view of tightening laws on the carriage of drugs (and some countries may impound even aspirin if you do not have a current prescription for it) great care should be exercised in this.

Whether or not alcohol should be included among the medicinal supplies is a moot point – there are those who insist that it has no place on board whatsoever. Its effects as a stimulant are short-lived but the greatest danger (discounting severe over-indulgence leading ultimately to a man overboard situation) is the onset of lassitude and a loss of concentration. But a tot in a mug of night-time cocoa is comforting and, when in harbour, a happy hour is a pleasant and relaxing way of celebrating safe arrival.

11 Planning & Paperwork

Almost any time except during the six weeks of high summer, it is quite realistic to simply hitch up, take to the open road and drive wherever fancy dictates, without any fixed itinerary, in this country at any rate. Admittedly, if trailing on the Continent, there will be a few formalities and also some unavoidable paperwork; at the time of writing, it does not appear that Britain's. membership of the European Community has simplified this at all! In late July and August, though, holiday crowding of launching and camping sites and in harbours and marinas does mean that at least some advance booking is advisable.

When working out the holiday route, several things need consideration but it is fair to say that for the majority of people the twin limiting factors will be those of time and money! These have a direct bearing on the distance travelled and possibly on the nature of the travelling, whether extended sailing or passage-making is to be considered, or whether the boat is to travel far afield on the trailer, possibly to be berthed in one spot and used for daysailing. This decision may rest to a large extent on the age and experience of the crew. Children are quickly bored and although they usually enjoy participation in the running of the boat, they soon tire of vast expanses of sea and beg for a change of scene. This is easier to lay on for their benefit when the boat is being trailed to the holiday destination but long periods cooped up in a car are also liable to pall.

With youngsters who have passed the fretful stage and are both keen and competent, more adventurous trips can be planned. First of all, an honest assessment of cruising speeds needs to be worked out – a reasonable working figure being in the region of four miles an hour at sea and thirty overland. It is obviously cheaper to make use of wind rather than the car's engine and quiet anchorages rather than marinas or camp sites. Accepting these figures as a guideline, a twenty-mile daily cruise, in settled weather, is quite possible, allowing time for a leisurely lunch and a swim. This fills an eight hour day quite nicely and means arriving in anchorage or harbour in the early evening with plenty of time to sample life ashore. True, in the Mediterranean, adhering closely to such a schedule might mean running the engine more than envisaged since the wind there is inclined to be light until midmorning when the sea breeze fills in, only to expire once again in the evening until the land breeze takes over. With an experienced crew and a vessel equipped for it, overnight cruising poses no difficulties – a passage of 100 miles during a 24 hour span is within the scope of the average 20 foot sailing boat.

On the road, assuming at least a major part of the journey to be over motorways or dual carriageways, ten times this distance is not out of the question – given a relay of drivers. Unless time is absolutely of the essence – perhaps when racing to catch a ferry sailing – a quite respectable day's drive would be 200 to 250 miles; this would be a total of about six hours at the wheel though this time would be interspersed with breaks to relax, perhaps a little sightseeing and a leisurely snack or two. This brings Ireland, Scotland and the Western Isles along with southern France, the Baltic and northern Spain easily within the compass of a 48 hour drive although many might wish to take a day or two longer to explore the countryside through which they travel.

Quite a bit of organisation is smoothed out if the boat is travelling to a race meeting. Prior arrangements will have been made for berthing and cranage (if necessary) and there will be willing hands to help with rigging and launching as well as an abundance of advice about restaurants, shops and local sites of interest – not even the keenest race all day, every day!

Going foreign

Going foreign is not at all a daunting proposition although it can appear to be so when maps, charts and forms are duly laid out for consultation. Manoeuvering a trailer down the ramp into the bowels of the ferry is nerve-wracking first time but anticipation is usually far worse than the reality. The marshals are helpful and, quite often the trailer is uncoupled and eased by them into the final position on the ship – although this is done mainly in the interest of loading as many vehicles on board as for the convenience of drivers. Allow a good margin of time at the ferry terminal: the operators reserve the right to inspect the gas installation.

Don't miss the tide: a Jaguar 21 on a custom trailer. The boat and trailer, in this case, will have to be unhitched from the tow vehicle and left to be floated free or eased down the slip under control from a winch mounted on the vehicle. The third alternative is to crane the yacht off, and in busy times, the crane may have to be pre-booked.

When cruising abroad, it is best to purchase all the charts required in this country; not only are they less expensive, they are easier to comprehend when written in English!

You should also take along pilot books for the projected sailing areas since these, when current, do provide the next best thing to local knowledge and should show launching sites, clubs, marinas and safe anchorages. If there are children along, it is worth knowing about any gentle shelving beaches where the yacht's shoal draft can be put to good use and they can simply paddle ashore. Indeed, it may even be worth planning the trip around one or two such beaches – though bathing beaches should be given a wide berth; even a slow-moving boat will not be welcome in the midst of swimmers and in some aras, may be the subject of an official reprimand.

An ideal first trip might well be down to the south of France, perhaps to the Languedoc/Roussillon region. Vast

sums of money have been spent to turn the rather uninterest-
ing coastal area into a yachtsman's paradise – but take
along plenty of insect repellent. Harbour facilities are first
class, and even in August it should be possible to find a
berth – though it is wisest to check this out in advance.

From Port Grimaud, La Grande Motte, or any one of the
adjacent yacht harbours, it is a short sail to Barcelona and
once there, for those embarking upon an offshore passage,
100 miles or so to the Balearics or even Corsica in the east. In
summer the winds are light (though it can blow hard and
from a clear sky, so consult the day's weather forecast posted
in the harbour office) and the beaches are beautiful and
uncrowded. Towards the end of August the mornings are
inclined to be misty but this sea fret disperses by midday and
the afternoons are then pleasantly warm.

The drive down from one of the Channel ports is hassle-
free once the Autoroute du Soleil is gained (try and circum-
navigate Paris in the quieter small hours of the morning) and
three days allow time to visit the wine-producing *chateaux*
country – the surrounding villages being liberally supplied
with parking areas and guest houses for those who wish to
make a pilgrimage to the vineyards rather than a passage
past them! The small towns themselves, though most pic-
turesque, have narrow and tortuous streets with
Machiavellian one way systems: I once thought I was condemned to spend the entire fortnight in Beaune and to this
day, have no clear recollection of how I eventually escaped!
(Death by dehydration was not imminent, however, as the
keepers of innumerable *caves* besieged the slow-moving car
and trailer with inducements to abandon both and sample
the local product.)

As a rule, if forays into towns are on the agenda, the most
sensible arrangement is to park the trailer, suitably protected
against theft, and proceed without it; in the majority of urban
centres, few of which were constructed for motor traffic, it is
hard enough to discover any space large enough to leave
even a car!

Denmark and southern Sweden are two other destinations
which should be considered. In the summer months the skies
are clear and the strong sun gives the lie to the inhospitable
reputation of the almost tideless Baltic. With enough time,
three weeks to a month perhaps, visit the Stockholm archi-
pelago consisting of myriad islands wooded with birch and
pine, some unoccupied, some with red-ochred barge-

boarded cottages on rocky outcrops and all reflected in waters of deepest aquamarine; a truly unforgettable area but watch out for the shoals of jellyfish. Enchanting as the region is, accurate navigation is a must; pilotage, too, must be precise as the buoys marking the deep water channels can be hard to pick out against the background of islands at times.

Driving to and launching from Kiel, perhaps after an overnight ferry sailing on the Harwich/Hamburg ferry is far less time-consuming than sailing outside the Danish coast or passing through the Kiel canal. This 50 mile waterway could not, by any stretch of the imagination, be described as welcoming to yachts and it is fair to say that for the smaller boat it can be actively dangerous. This is because of the amount of commercial shipping; theoretically it is subject to an 8 knot speed limit but many skippers choose to ignore it. A couple of rogue coasters passing at speed (and they do) will create a

An E boat on a tilting trailer en route for Switzerland where the width of a load trailed behind a light motor vehicle is restricted. As the trailer is tilted about its axis, the beam of the boat is effectively reduced – though winching it back onto the level for camping onboard involves much heaving! Although the load appears out of balance, there is no marked difference from the driver's point of view – but it does raise official eyebrows.

wash which could send a trailer sailer out of control, causing it to either go aground or crash into one of the substantial dolphins along the edge of the bank. The approach from the River Elbe is also very congested – and, in the entry and exit locks to and from the canal, the law of the jungle prevails.

For a 20-foot boat, the North Sea crossing to Holland, even at its shortest direct point, may not be altogether an enticing prospect but that country, its canals, and in particular the Ijsselmeer are a fine area for a holiday cruise, rarely over-crowded and endlessly fascinating even in mist, drizzle or rain – all of which are sure to be provided lavishly. The Ijsselmeer, the large inland sea formed when the Zuyder Zee was dammed some forty years ago, can kick up a short steep sea and, as landmarks are difficult to distinguish, one from another, some chartwork is called for. But shores are set about with historic towns, perhaps a little self-consciously parading their history for tourists, but delightful nonetheless.

Those more venturesome, or with more time to spend, might well be tempted by the longer drive down through Italy and thence by ferry from Brindisi. Greece and the islands of the Aegean are all within reach even if one summer's cruising would serve only to whet the appetite for more.

Advance booking

In few countries does overnight parking for car and trailer pose problems. On the Continent, at least on major tourist routes, there are laybys in plenty, set out with picnic tables and chairs and often boasting loos and washing facilities. Don't leave it until the last minute at weekends, though, as the entire population of each country apparently takes to its wheels at 4 pm on Friday. Camp site superintendents have widely differing reactions to the sight of a trailer sailer seeking accommodation; in the low season, so long as there is room to wedge the object into a convenient space, they are only too delighted, in summer they may throw up their hands in horror! As they may, incidentally, if there is an all-male or all-female party on board; some camp sites ban any such groups regardless, though many will accept them if informed at the time of booking. It is wiser to book in advance, stating the unorthodox nature of trailer and its overall length. Consider joining the Camping Club of Great Britain if you do plan to use camp sites, and obtain a camping carnet from the AA, even though this is not mandatory. The motoring organisations are most useful when it comes to sorting out the paperwork for a trip abroad. Requirements do vary from country to country but in all cases you must have proof of the car insurance and it is best to have a green card. In your own interest too, you really should have informed the insurance company of car and boat – or both if policies are not held by the same insurers – just to make certain that they are aware the boat is to be trailed: establish that any damage to the boat, whether on the road or during the launch/recovery is fully covered. (The boat's insurers must of course be informed of the sailing area intended and may make a small additional charge for this.) Third party insurance is compulsory when sailing in Italian waters, also for the Swiss lakes and is, nowadays, usually demanded by all marinas and yacht harbours. Personal insurance should also be considered though there are reciprocal arrangements for medical aid throughout the EEC (complete DSS form E111 beforehand).

An international driving licence is suggested even for the EEC countries where it is not strictly necessary, and there are circumstances in which it would be useful also to have your current British one (if for any reason it may be necessary to hire a car or motorcycle, for instance). For those holding the older style green driving licences, a translation is advisable when visiting Spain – as is a bail bond, as participants in a serious motoring accident may otherwise find themselves in prison.

More likely than a serious accident is a breakdown. Even a minor malfunction can upset schedules and weeks of prior planning but a mishap such as disintegration of engine or gearbox, in particular where the car is of a comparatively rare marque, can be financially ruinous. But here, too, the motoring associations can be of service: they offer comprehensive insurance against just about everything under the sun: cover can be taken out to include vehicle collection and recovery, hotel bills and economy flights home in an emergency and also the assistance of an alternative driver should illness strike down the one who normally takes the wheel. The policies are far from expensive considering the extent of the benefits, with the most comprehensive on offer covering boat, trailer and passengers; these work out at somewhere in the region of 5% of the basic holiday price. Some of these policies, though, are not available to vehicles over ten years old; do establish what is offered before signing the contract.

Ship's papers

Registration of the boat is not as yet universally compulsory, but in all likelihood it soon will be and is most strongly recommended. If your vessel is not registered as a British ship, the cost of full, formal registration will almost certainly be prohibitive. It entails production of a builder's certificate, difficult in any case with an older boat, checking that the name is not duplicated by any other registered vessel and also rather complex measurement of the hull. It is arguably worthwhile as a guarantee of ownership and permission to carry bonded stores. If interested, the Customs and Excise of the nearest port of registry will supply full details. The usual alternative is that of the SSR (Small Ships Register) which is adequate for foreign travel. The fee is very reasonable and the document remains valid for five years or until change of ownership. The register is administered by the DVLA, Swansea SA99 1BX, telephone: 0792 783355.

There may be a need for a Customs bond or carnet: this varies according to country and at the time of writing, beaurocracy is in what can only be described as a state of flux. Belgium still demands a carnet for boats over 5.5 m in length and all powered craft – Finland and Hungary even for canoes and inflatables of this length or over. Turkey and Luxembourg insist on them for everything that floats, and Morocco for all power boats. The best advice is to check with the RYA a few weeks before setting off. If a carnet does prove to be an essential addition to the documents, the AA can supply one. But if one has been issued to you, do be careful not to lose, give away or abandon *any* part of the yacht or its inventory. In your own interest, notify the police immediately if any item is stolen, especially if it is the outboard; failure to do so can cause official fury of truly awesome proportions. This I found out to my cost when I lent an outboard to a Spanish friend whose own had broken down, and I returned briefly to England with the boat but no engine: I was relentlessly pursued for nearly two years until the outboard was returned to Britain and the paperwork completed.

Don't forget your passport – and those of the crew. In EEC countries it is rare for them to be subjected to scrutiny but there are random checks in order to counter terrorism, the drugs traffic and rabies.

Recommended for anyone taking a powered craft anywhere in Europe is a Helmsman's Certificate of Competence: this will almost certainly be demanded by those embarking upon the inland waterways and, in Italy, it will be expected to be produced by anyone operating a motor or sail boat. Once again, the RYA should be contacted for details and the application form.

Whether or not the provision of money for the holiday venture could be construed as paperwork is perhaps, debatable, although traveller's cheques and Eurocheques do have to be ordered in advance (as will a Eurocheque card if one is not already in your possession). Identification will usually be required on encashment of either type so have the passport with you when visiting the bank (and make certain there is at least one safe place to keep it and all other valuables on board the boat – everyone has a favourite hiding place but it would hardly be in the interests of crime prevention to list the more ingenious ones in this book!

The idea of the Common Market is that there will be no more violent fluctuations between European currencies, though cynics might be convinced of this only after several years of the ECU. Exchange rate monitoring is therefore, likely to remain a popular pastime for the foreseeable future and the results of gambling on the advantages of traveller's cheques in various currencies a subject for much after-dinner bragging. Apart from the large denomination notes – which will in any case be swallowed all too quickly by the sundries of life afloat and onshore, remember to keep a supply of coin for the autoroute tolls – the toll booths on certain Continental motorways appear on the horizon with remarkable frequency and their fees can seriously damage your wallet.

One facet of forward planning in fact is to calculate the difference in cost between driving unconcernedly along the excellent surfaces of the direct motorway links – with tolls – and tackling the dubious cobbles and pockmarked blacktop of secondary routes without tolls. Take into consideration such things as wear on tyres, tempers and suspension; time lost through seeking (absent) signposts, detours and roadworks and the increased petrol consumption entailed by tortuous by-roads which, in spite of reassurance by local worthies lead only to derelict farms or a sewage treatment unit.

Don't forget either, that the majority of back roads are not much blessed with petrol stations – let alone ones which open in early morning or evening.

When examining the basics, there is little doubt that the most important pieces of paper to have with you always are those which fold and rustle; still, in the interests of a peaceful and untroubled holiday, it is probably best not to overlook the need for the formal documents!

12 The Elements of Seamanship

Seamanship, it is said, can be learned but not taught – certainly it cannot be taught, or even explained, in a few pages of print. Formal instruction does however, have a vital part in the learning process, even though it could be argued that it often concentrates too much on teaching how to get out of situations that no seaman should have got into in the first place! Cynical as this attitude is, it is widely held, and with some truth.

It must seem a foregone conclusion that no-one would go to sea without chart and compass, a reasonable knowledge of boat handling in all wind and sea states, of navigation and pilotage: also at least sufficient experience to understand the procedure for entering harbour, the right way to moor and anchor and how to deal with such mishaps as running aground. That people do, indeed, go to sea sadly lacking in such knowledge is borne out by the rescue services although, to be honest, not all the culprits are yachtsmen.

But, even though experience counts for much, a week's intensive sailing course at a reputable school will provide a sound basis upon which to build. Then sail – get out on the water in everything possible, from racing dinghies (which work wonders for stamina and balance) to large yachts and even square riggers if the opportunity presents itself. When sailing your own boat, even for an afternoon, try to have a definite objective: head for a certain anchorage, perhaps with a fixed time of arrival in mind, lay off the course, take bearings on everything, keep the log and, in effect, make a mini-cruise of it. Practise heaving-to, experiment with self-steering by the set of the sails, practise man-overboard drill and picking up buoys: in warm weather at least a degree of amusement can be extracted from this. And practise anchoring – quite a few yachts of all sizes these days sail only from marina to marina, which probably explains why their ground tackle is so often woefully inadequate.

Severe weather is generally considered the greatest menace to small boats: this is taken to mean winds of force 7 (around 30 knots) and upwards, but in a wind over tide situa-

Small boats, such as this 19 foot Carina, are slowed down markedly in a heavy swell.

tion, 20 knots dead on the nose will be quite enough to rattle the average trailer sailer. Some designs are better suited to plugging on in bad weather, but as a rule, there is only a relatively small 'weather window' within which the very smallest boats, 18 ft or so, can safely plan to sail. Below force 2 there is not breeze enough to achieve anything like the maximum waterline speed: in winds of over force 5, the boat may simply not have enough lateral resistance to overcome the windage of her hull and rig, and so will not make any measurable headway to windward at all. This does not necessarily imply that the crew is exposed to any great risk but it does suggest that no-one should ever set off without an alternative protected harbour or anchorage within reach, should the wind pipe up or change direction. (Ensure charts and pilot books are on board!)

Weather wise

Careful attention to weather forecasts, backed up with regular checks of the ship's barometer (which should always be on board) do, in most instances, give sufficient advance warning of a deteriorating weather pattern but sooner or later, most yachts will come in for a dusting. It can be alarming, of that there is no doubt, but given confidence in the boat and skipper and enough sea room to sit the gale out, bad weather in itself should not hazard the vessel. But there are two very real dangers – one is simple fear, exacerbated often by seasickness and the noise of the wind itself. The other is failure of part of the vessel's equipment: dismasting does occur from time to time and early reefing is essential, particularly in those boats with high-aspect lightly-sparred fractional rigs.

Engines, too, frequently cease to function when most needed; this is often the result of sediment stirred up in the fuel – or in the case of an outboard, repeated dousing in salt water. A sheet or warp may, unnoticed, wrap itself round the propeller, so check that all ropes' ends are secure – especially in a boat with an open or cut-away transom. In the event of a knock-down, rare, though not by any means unknown in a yacht caught unawares with sheets pinned, there is always the chance of losing a hatch. All too often, cockpit lockers are vast and, though this is not always apparent at first glance, drain directly into the main bilges so that the loss of a lid could result in total inundation of the boat. Rudders are occasionally carried away, though it should immediately be possible to steady the boat with a bucket on a long scope trailed over the stern (but beware of fouling the prop if the engine is running).

Know your boat

Familiarity with the behaviour of the boat under various combinations of rig and widely ranging wind strengths does instil confidence. It is very debatable whether any boat should deliberately put out in a gale but if there is an opportunity to do so in sheltered waters, it may be worth the risk.

There is one fear perhaps more insistent than that of meeting a gale head-on. It is that of being run down by a larger vessel. Even in these days of sophisticated radar, it is not to be lightly dismissed. No small boat in anything of a seaway can expect to be clearly visible from the bridge of a ship – and the radar echo, not strong in the first place, may be virtually lost in the wave clutter.

Night sailing

Night sailing experience is vital and should be gained in waters familiar to you and, when on passage, never leave anyone on watch unless you are certain that they understand the significance of all the navigation lights which will be in evidence around. Make certain too, that their eyesight – and your own for that matter – is trustworthy; defects of vision are usually more pronounced in darkness or poor light. That said, navigating at night is no more difficult than in the daytime; when looking seawards, lighted buoys are easier to spot and identify although making sense of clusters of leading, warning and entry lights in the vicinity of a large harbour does take a bit of practice. Distances can be deceptive: what may seem to be the powerful flashing light of a buoy a mile or so distant may approach with startling speed and be revealed as a channel marker close under the bow. This is a particular danger on very dark nights when the structure of the buoy or beacon cannot easily be distinguished from the surrounding night.

Do not assume that because there are no lights visible there are no buoys or ships in the offing, marker lights do fail and, though they should not do so, at times vessels proceed without lights, especially boats which are engaged in illegal fishing.

To a large extent, the safety of the yacht at night depends on the navigation lights, their power and location, and on the state of the battery (few small yachts rely on paraffin). A masthead tri-colour light is undoubtedly superior but if there is a bad connection or break in the wire little can be done to rectify it at night. Therefore it is not a bad idea to maintain a back-up system with lights mounted on coachroof or pulpit (or carry dry-battery portable lights which can be clipped to the standing rigging). Although not everyone is in favour of them, I always fit spreader lights or a deck floodlight in spite of the power they devour, since the strong white light will be visible when coloured lights might not be.

There should be a white flare to hand in the cockpit (in current date for use) if there seems an imminent risk of collision but don't use one (or the spreader lights or searchlight) at the very last minute, or there is a chance that the watchkeeper of the approaching vessel will be startled into altering course through 90%, thus bringing about the very collision you have been trying to avoid.

Equally, when in the vicinity of other shipping, do not make abrupt changes to your own course. This might just initiate a series of evasive manoeuvres which could cause a deeper draft ship to run aground or collide, either with you or with another craft nearby. If the wind starts to die, a sailing boat without auxiliary power may have a worrying time of it, so do ensure that there is a white flare or torch within grasp and have an oar or paddle handy so that you can at least put the yacht on to the opposite tack. In congested shipping lanes, especially those where pilot cutters, patrol boats and dredgers work in an apparently random fashion, a motionless yacht may simply not be noticed by other lookouts and, unable to take any avoiding action, will be at some considerable risk.

Coping with fog

Fog compounds the difficulties. It distorts any lights which may be visible and muffles and alters sounds, though it should, nevertheless, be possible to hear the vibrations of a large screw from about a mile away. There is almost a classic 'Catch 22' situation for any yacht: without the engine, it may not be possible to get clear of a ship coming up – with it running, you will almost certainly not be aware of such an approach.

Having of course, meticulously plotted your own boat's position (or consulted the GPS) you will know exactly where you are even in the fog – though this may not impart a great deal of comfort. Probably the safest plan is to head for shallower water where it should be possible to drop anchor, secure at least in the knowledge that nothing of any great size can thunder into your boat as it will run aground first. At all costs try not to strand yourself; after fog, the wind may rise and you will be in a potentially hazardous situation. As long as the fog lasts, have one member of crew on watch sounding the horn at two-minute intervals. Half an hour's watch per person is long enough, as staring into featureless space plays havoc with imagination and eyesight.

On gaining a known area of safe shoal water, some relaxation is in order but until then, have the crew in lifejackets, on the coachroof, ready with flares, and, if there is a dinghy, stream it astern with water and a few necessities stowed securely in it. Should there be no shallow water nearby, hold the original course at low speed, making due allowance for tidal sets, for these affect the course made good far more when the yacht is moving only slowly. It is rare for fog to blanket an area for longer than four or five hours without the slightest lift and, should one occur, take the opportunity to establish or confirm a position rather than making an attempt to dodge into an unfamiliar harbour. There is a good chance that the improvement may only be local and, should the fog close in again, you could be worse off than before. In all honesty, when fog descends there is little to be done to improve the situation; it is a case of being patient, keeping as alert as possible, and waiting for things to change.

Tactics in gale conditions

Much the same holds true if caught out in a gale though the motion will be violent and the boat moving faster, possibly towards a hazardous lee shore. This latter possibility is the stuff of which dramas are made, and not without reason as a hostile coastline has reduced many a vessel to matchwood. There are early warning signs which are rarely absent: thin high cirrus cloud streaming like tattered banners towards the horizon with cumulus below it, a fall in the barometer (and it does tend to be true that a rapid fall foretells an imminent but short-lived gale while a steady drop is the precursor of an impending protracted blow). Of course, there are the invaluable radio weather forecasts, which should be monitored. Once a gale warning is issued, the urge to head for the nearest haven becomes almost irresistible, and yet it must be resisted. In a rising gale, the safety of any harbour to leeward is far outweighed by the risk entailed in approaching and entering it. As history recounts, far more boats have been lost a stone's throw from their home port than on the open sea.

As the wind strengthens, reduce main and headsail progressively, to maintain the balance of the rig, and try to make up to windward. If necessary, run the engine to assist – the offing may be invaluable later on. Eventually the point will come when the sails flog more than they drive and forward progress comes to a shuddering halt.

This is the moment of decision. Can you now turn and reach shelter in the lee of a headland? Would you, in fact, be safe there if the wind backed? And would you bet your life on it? Alarmist though this may sound, it could, in essence, be

Fig 11
Lying hove-to with headsail partially furled and set aback and the main reefed and eased away. It takes a while to achieve the best sail trim in order to lie quietly; some yachts with high freeboard and shallow forefoot may need a constant hand at the helm. Keep the main hatch shut (but be certain that anyone down below is able to open it), wear a life-jacket, and keep your lifeline attached as near the centreline of the yacht as possible. Keep flares, including a white flare, to hand, and have a torch ready. Keep a close watch for shipping, especially for ships approaching from astern which may have great difficulty in seeing a small yacht. Bear in mind that weather which overpowers a small boat will not necessarily have the same effect on a large yacht, which may revel in the tough-going. Yachts can be an unexpected danger as they are silent, and unfortunately the watchkeeping cannot always be absolutely relied upon. Keep a flask of soup or coffee handy; a rationed sip every twenty minutes helps the time pass!

what it amounts to. If there exists the merest shadow of a doubt, now is the time to heave-to. As you do this, make a note of the time, take bearings on such marks as may be visible and try to fix a position. Allow for the drift, which may be as much as $1^1/2$–2 knots to leeward; bear in mind also that there will be a slight forward motion, and do not forget to check tidal streams.

Little difficulty is encountered in persuading most yachts to heave-to; the trouble, most pronounced, unfortunately, in light boats which lack forefoot and long keels, is getting them to remain hove-to for more than a few minutes. This is where experimenting before you need it pays dividends. Generally a balance between backed foresail and reefed, eased mainsail can be established, though a few boats will lie peacefully enough under backed headsail alone. Often a light boat will need a guiding hand on the tiller to prevent it being thrown around too much by wave action; most craft tend to head up slightly and then fall away, and as a result the sails are subjected to unavoidable flogging. If a storm jib and tri-sail are on board, this is an occasion to set them.

Oddly enough, the motion is not quite as uncomfortable for the crew as might be expected – in fact it often comes as something of a relief. But the moment may arrive, if the gale continues to rise, when it is best to get all sail off and lie a'hull, and this can be decidedly unpleasant as the boat will lie beam-on to the waves and roll abominably. Everything that can be lashed into place, must be. A keen lookout must be kept for other vessels in the vicinity; without sails the yacht will be unable to take any avoiding action. Once again, so long as there is plenty of searoom, there is little actual danger; it is mainly a case of sitting things out. After the first hour or two the stirrings of panic tend to die away (though the risk is that they may be replaced by a feeling of lethargy) and if the crew can take at least liquid (non-alcoholic) nourishment, they should try to. You may, however, offer up a few earnest prayers and wonder whether mowing the lawn on Sundays was really as dull as all that!

It used to be the exception rather than the rule for a severe and long-lived gale to strike the British coastline in summer, but weather patterns seem to have changed and from time to time storms do occur which are of sufficient severity to cause seas so steep and broken that no yacht can life safely a'hull without running an unacceptable risk of being rolled. If there is such a sea, the normal procedure suggested is to run off before it, under bare poles and with warps trailed astern to steady the vessel and in the optimistic hopes of disturbing wavecrests before they can wash on board. Since most smaller craft are sailing in coastal waters with land under the lee bow, this option may not be available – hence the urgent need to gain an offing as soon as the weather deteriorates.

Anchoring in exposed waters is really the last resort if the shoreline is close and all else fails. But good ground tackle may hold, and there is a better than even chance that it will buy enough time for flares to be sent up, and help to arrive.

It should be stressed that the likelihood of encountering survival conditions in the course of normal cruising is not

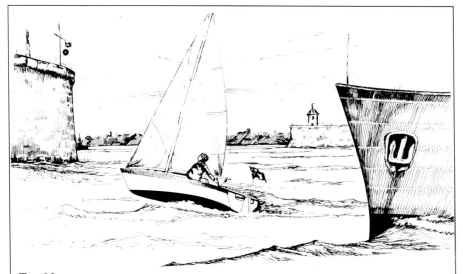

Fig 12
Entering harbour. Approaching an unfamiliar harbour – especially under sail – is often a more unnerving than a pleasurable experience. It is difficult to judge the effects of an off-shore breeze which may tend to blow in fitful gusts within the harbour walls – that is, when it does not die completely. Be chary of approaching the harbour wall so closely that it is impossible to see around it: local boats may be waiting en masse for their permission to leave harbour (and if they are fishing vessels, Heaven help anything in their path!). Fenders should be made ready for an instant drop on both sides of the yacht, mooring warps should lead outside all, with a heaving line made up and coiled to throw if necessary.Concentrate on sailing and don't let the usual crowd of onlookers on the pierhead put you off. Beware of anglers' fishing lines and look astern occasionally … that entry signal may not be just for you alone!

high but the situation can occur. It is incumbent upon all who skipper a yacht to have equipped the boat accordingly and to have at least formulated plans for dealing with bad weather conditions.

Entering a new harbour

To a more pleasant subject: entering a new harbour. The excitement, the interest, the slight frisson of the unknown (since past experience may remind you that what is shown on the large scale chart may not necessarily bear much resemblance to what is actually hidden by the encircling wall). Little of real menace in the majority of cases, fishing boats, fast power craft and dredgers being the commonest and, so long as these have obeyed the port signals, all should be waiting upon your grand entrance – as undoubtedly will the harbour master, receipt book in hand!

Make the approach without undue haste, ensure that enough fenders are positioned, that warps are led correctly, heaving lines coiled and free of kinks (and that none are able to slip surreptitiously overboard to foul the prop). It is more usual, in these days of heavy harbour traffic, for even a nimble sailing vessel to make use of the engine rather than sail in, but it is never wise to stow sails with their covers on: have them clear to hoist at a moment's notice.

If not directed to a berth, be prepared to lie alongside either the harbour wall or another boat. Where there is a choice in the matter, a yacht, only slightly larger than your own and with freeboard of a not too dissimilar height is best (especially if it seems as though the owners have decamped for the week).

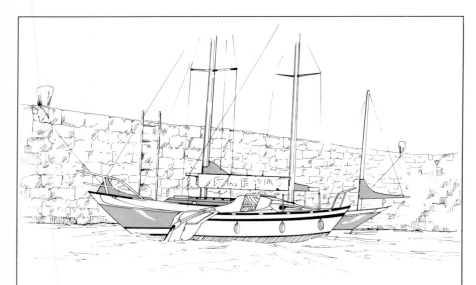

Fig 13
Lying alongside in harbour. Try to find a yacht with freeboard similar in height to your own, but check that your stanchions and spreaders won't foul those of your neighbour in a swell or wash. If possible, try to moor bows to stern and always tread carefully when crossing any boat alongside; use the foredeck rather than tramping across the cockpit or coachroof – and bear in mind that there may be a tired crew attempting to get their heads down after a long passage. Take mooring lines ashore; there should only be a spring and possibly a breast rope on the boat alongside. Have adequate sized fenders out on both sides, and be prepared to move if necessary either to allow the neighbouring boat to move off or to accommodate a larger boat which may have no option but to raft up.

Take bow and stern warps to the shore with just springs and breast ropes secured to the new neighbour. Once settled, make sure that stanchions, if angled outwards, cannot become entangled with those of the other vessel in a swell. This also applies to crosstrees and spreaders. If your fenders are too small to keep both yachts safely clear of each other, lash two or three together into a bundle.

There may be no alternative to mooring alongside a quay though this is rarely the most comfortable of berths. In tidal waters, before mooring for any length of time it must be established whether the yacht will take the ground towards low water – also whether there are any ledges or obstructions which could damage the hull: if you turn up late at night, there may be no-one around able to confirm or deny this. In case of doubt, there is nothing else for it but to move. If all aspects are favourable, yet there is one slot, enticingly vacant – suspect the presence of a sewage outfall or the imminent arrival of the trawler fleet. Where there is any measurable tidal range, warps must be tended regularly, neither can it be assumed that the fenders will be proof against all evils: many harbour walls are constructed of heavy concrete or steel pilings and smaller sized fenders can catch in between these – a wooden spar hung outboard will guard against this. In a commercial harbour where grit, grease and muck abound and can be ground into the topsides, fender aprons, oblongs of canvas or PVC eyeletted at the corners, can be slung inboard of the fenders and should offer a fair degree of protection to the gel or paintwork.

If the harbour does dry, even though the ground may not be foul, special care is called for. It is unwise to lie alongside another vessel, even a larger one, since draft is not easy to estimate. That convenient 80-foot lighter may draw less than your own boat, and if the seabed slopes away from the wall, might slide outwards pinning your smaller boat partly beneath it. If the rudder can easily be removed do so, take the outboard off, too, if you can, as a warp fouling it may rip engine and bracket off the transom. Care must be taken to adjust the mooring lines immediately prior to the boat taking the ground since the boat must not be allowed to drift away from the wall as it touches. If this does happen, the boat must be heeled towards the wall (since the cockpit might fill with water if the list is outwards and down any incline), but heavy stress will be taken by the shrouds; this could possibly result in the loss of the mast.

Running aground

Although beaching for a scrub on a summer's day is one aspect of routine maintenance which can be enjoyable, providing, as it does, a handy excuse for a beach party, running aground unintentionally can be a blessed nuisance. Moreover, it is all too often readily apparent to all those sailing merrily past (those who did keep religiously to the dredged channel!). Mostly it happens due to overstanding a tack, and when the tide is falling there may be an undesirable suggestion of permanence. Should the tides be falling off after high springs, this permanence may become an accomplished fact and a grounding ocurring at such times can be truly regarded as an emergency.

Running hard ashore on an exposed sandbank in worsening weather also has ample potential for disaster: the yacht may literally pound to pieces. Prompt action may save the day but it must be so prompt as to be instinctive. Tacking immediately, headsail aback to spin the boat on its axis, may be action enough – it almost certainly will be in the case of a bilge-keeler which would most likely be heeled at the moment of touching the putty and will therefore draw less as the hull comes upright.

The reverse, sad to say, is true of a single-fin keeled boat, although with some racing designs the draft can be reduced slightly if the crew crowd together on the snout. If this, or increasing the angle of heel by ordering some unfortunate to sit on the clew outhaul of the main boom, does not achieve the desired effect of swinging the boat clear, it will be necessary to start the engine and reverse off. Without an engine, a touch of feverish poling and paddling will be urgently required.

If the boat is a lift-keeler, the answer is obvious – start lifting, winding the winch as though there will be no tomorrow. Bring the rudder up at the same time, progressively. If there is nothing to steer with, another appointment with the mud is on the cards. If all else fails, as a last resort a selfless hand had better be dispatched over the side to physically heave the boat free. The success or otherwise of this move naturally depends on the depth of the water and the state of the bottom: three feet of water and mud will make it impossible for him to keep his balance, let alone attempt any strong arm stuff. Assuming all the effort to be successful, however, the crew person had better rejoin the boat without delay before it moves downwind!

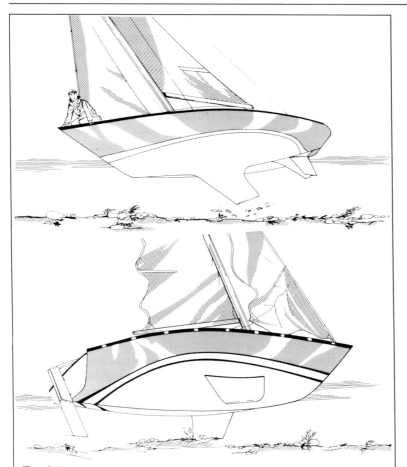

Fig 14

a Running aground. Yachts with a single centreline fin keel draw less when heeled (and most groundings do take place when over-standing a tack working up a narrow tidal channel). Try, therefore, to keep the boat at an angle and sail off, rather than luffing to a standstill and wasting minutes getting the engine started: on a falling tide, there won't be sufficient time. Some light keelboats draw less with the crew perched in the eyes of the boat, otherwise get their combined weight as far outboard as possible, on the boom outhaul if necessary. In the case of a lift keel boat – start winching – fast! Take care, though, not to retract keel and rudder totally or the boat will simply blow downwind and then be in worse trouble than before!

b Bilge keelers draw more when heeled, so take a deep breath and try to sail back, sheets eased, on a reciprocal course! If all else fails, in a shallow draft boat, it may be feasible for one of the crew to go over the side and unstick the boat by some judicious shoving. Don't attempt this unless you know the type of bottom, the fitness of the crew, and whether you can haul him or her back on board again afterwards.

If it looks as though there is nothing which can be done to get the boat off, put on a brave face and pretend that inspection of the underbody was recommended by your surveyor. Some precautions, though, must be taken against decreasing tidal heights and/or deteriorating weather. First and foremost, if the boat has grounded on the edge of an incline, ensure that it is not going to tip the wrong way and fall into deeper water. Take the bower anchor out as far to windward as possible and, once again, await developments – if the wait is going to be a protracted one, try and snatch some rest.

Man overboard

Although sailing life is, on the whole, adequately provided with fears and alarms – most of which turn out to be just that and no more – everyone who sails with friends or family (and doubtless those who sail alone too, though they might fight shy of admitting it) has a terror of losing someone overboard. In spite of guardwires, safety harnesses, jackstays and the exercise of utmost caution, it still does happen. And if it happens at night, the chances of survival and recovery are lessened, possibly just because no-one will be aware of it happening. All yachts should practise man overboard drill but because most sail with different crews on board, not all will be conversant with it. This is regrettably true (though less so in recent years) in family crewed boats, where the skipper may be the only one with any real expertise in boat handling and may also carry out most of the deck work. Thus, ironically, it happens that the one person who probably could cope with such an emergency is the very one who is the victim of it.

If somebody does go over, the immediate action is to throw a lifebuoy (which should have a light and/or a floating line attached). Then *quickly* get the vessel on to a reciprocal course. Gybing is usually advocated since it places the yacht downwind of the swimmer, and on turning it should come head to wind near to him. But, instant gybing is not always possible if the main is vanged out or if there are running backstays to be freed off, for example. If possible avoid running the engine because of the risk of injury by the propeller.

Once the casualty has been located, some of the immediate panic generated by the situation is generally dissipated: the crew member is there, alive. Now it remains only to bring him or her back on board. If the person is still capable of self-help, this should not be too difficult, though constant reassurance may be needed until arrangements have been made. A boarding ladder at the stern seems the obvious way to retrieve someone who has gone over the side, but after surprisingly few minutes in the water, strength seems to flag, partly sapped by the initial shock, and he may not make it unaided. If there is no boarding ladder, a bight or rope will serve the same purpose; it will at least provide a foothold and a breathing space, and allow water to drain from clothing.

Bringing an unconscious or totally exhausted victim aboard is far more difficult, especially if it has to be done single-handed. The first action must be to get a line under the armpits and at least keep his head clear of the water. If the boat is rolling beam on it may then be possible, once the guardwires· have been cut (the reason why guardwires should be set up with lashings rather than rigging screws), to allow the action of the boat to do the work, using a winch to maintain tension on the line. It may even prove necessary to lower the mainsail, free the luff from the mast and, with the boom lashed in place, drop the sail into the water, halyard still secured to head: this will make a sling into which the person can scramble. Sling and occupant can then be hauled or winched inboard, slowly, for water must be allowed to drain.

An inflatable dinghy, possibly better only partially inflated, performs the same task very well indeed. Even when the casualty has been located – and, in the dark and without an exact idea of the time the incident took place, this may take a considerable period of time, it may still take another half hour or so before he can be finally brought on board. Within the space of that half-hour there is a real chance of hypothermia, although almost any form of personal buoyancy will reduce this risk; not only does it add some bodily warmth but also minimises the need to struggle just to remain afloat. Each and every crew member should be provided with a lifejacket (rather than trusting merely to a buoyancy aid) – but choose one which is light and flexible or the temptation may simply be not to wear it. It should be equipped with a light (regularly checked), and a whistle. I am also very much in favour of carrying mini-flares, particularly if sailing any distance offshore and out of season.

Falling overboard is, of course, the happening most dreaded by any single-hander. To lie, floating helpless in the water while the yacht sails blithely on, the autopilot directing it ever further away, is truly the stuff of nightmares. Once at sea, and away from crowded waters, trailing a line of at least thirty feet in length with some form of handhold at the end does give the man overboard a chance to catch up with the boat, and the weight on the stern should override the autopilot or self-steering. If there is a transom-hung rudder, the pintles may be enough to gain a foothold, but clearly a boarding ladder or folding steps are preferable, though even with these, regaining the cockpit may not be easy. The most immediate necessity is to secure a bight of rope around the body (or clip on the safety harness if worn) so that there is no risk of falling back once again.

There are other perils which can strike – and most skippers suffer these in the imagination with monotonous regularity (though this is no bad thing – so long as the solutions to all emergencies are also worked out!). Accidents can more or less be relegated to the world of the imagination, though, given that the boat is well-equipped and maintained and that the crew, even if not super-fit, is at least well fed and rested. Assuming this to be the case the boat should come through most things unscathed – except possibly a fire or explosion on board. It is a terrible tragedy when, as happens far too often, a boat is found floating and undamaged but the crew, having taken to a liferaft, are never seen again. It makes excellent sense to buy or hire a liferaft if cruising offshore, since there are, of course, catastrophes which no yacht could ever hope to survive. But a well-found boat can survive most things, sometimes in spite of the crew rather than because of it. There is a strong temptation to take to a liferaft simply because it is there, but it is wrong to assume automatically that is the safest alternative. It isn't: stay with your ship if you possibly can. When all is said and done it is – and always will be – the best of all possible friends.

Appendix
Trailer Regulations

These regulations are correct at time of press but no responsibility or liability can be accepted for subsequent alterations and amendments.

Dimensions/projections

Trailer length, if towed by a car (as opposed to a goods vehicle) should not exceed 7 metres overall (excluding the hitch). Maximum permitted width is 2.3 metres.

If the total width is in excess of 2.9 metres the police must be informed in advance, if the total width exceeds 3.5 metres the police must be informed and a driver's assistant carried. The maximum width allowed is 4.3 metres.

No load to project more than 305 mm from the side of trailer, total width of trailer and any sideways overhang must not exceed 2.9 metres.

There is no stipulated maximum height limit but clearly load distribution and balance – also low bridges etc do impose a practical limitation.

Rearward projections in excess of 1 metre must be marked so as to be clearly visible (a red or orange streamer or bag for example). If the rearward projection is between 2 and 3.05 metres it must be fitted with an approved end marker board (a triangle with two sides of equal length, base and height to be of not less than 610 mm, the board to be painted with alternating red and white stripes). If the projection is beyond 3.05 metres, there must also be two side marker boards, the police must be informed in advance and a driver's assistant carried along.

Any projection must be protected so as to prevent infliction of harm or damage. The propeller blades of an outboard engine carried on the transom are regarded as particularly hazardous and should be wrapped or lagged and covered by a high visibility bag.

Trailer specifications

These terms are used in the regulations (Road vehicles, Construction and Use) to define weights pertaining to road trailers:

 i *Axle Weight* the sum of the weights transmitted to the road surface by that axle.

ii *Gross Weight* (a) in relation to a motor vehicle: this is the sum of the weight transmitted to the road surface by all the wheels of the vehicle.

(b) in relation to a trailer: this is the sum of all the weights transmitted to the road surface by all the wheels of the trailer and of any weight of the trailer imposed upon the tow vehicle.

iii *Maximum Gross Weight* (a) in the case of a trailer with a rating plate: the maximum gross weight shown on that plate.

(b) in all other cases: the weight which the trailer is designed (or adapted) not to exceed when travelling on the road.

iv *Kerb (kerbside) Weight* (a) in the case of a motor vehicle: the weight without passengers but with normal tools (jack, wheelbrace etc) and a full tank of fuel.

(b) in the case of a trailer: the unladen weight.

v *Laden Weight/Gross Weight* in the case of a trailer: both mean the unladen (kerb) weight of the trailer plus the carried load.

Unbraked trailers must be marked with the maximum gross weight, in a conspicuous place on the nearside. If in doubt, take the trailer to a local weighbridge!

Brakes

Trailers must be fitted with type approved brakes and a parking brake capable of holding the trailer on an 18 per cent gradient if:

i The sum of the trailer's designed axle weight is in excess of 750 kg.

ii The laden weight exceeds the maximum gross weight.

iii The laden weight of the trailer exceeds half of the tow vehicle's kerb weight.

Trailers first used before 1 April 1983 may have overrun or inertia brakes which apply automatically if the trailer overruns. Trailers first used after that date may also be fitted with overrun brakes but couplings must be damped and matched with brake linkage.

Trailers manufactured after 1 April 1989 must be fitted with an 'auto-reverse' braking system (which obviates the need for manual operation of a reversing catch prior to backing the trailer).

A trailer should be fitted with an emergency device to bring it to a halt should it become uncoupled from the tow vehicle. (This does not apply to single axle trailers of up to 1500 kg maximum gross weight so long as they are provided with a chain or cable capable of preventing the coupling head from touching the ground in the event of accidental uncoupling).

Lighting

All trailers, irrespective of the size or the age *must* have:

  i 2 rear red position lights,
  ii 2 rear red stop lights,
  iii 2 rear red retro-reflectors (not more than 400 mm from the sides of the trailer),
  iv rear white number plate light or lights.

Trailers manufactured after 1 September 1965 must, in addition have two rear amber direction indicators.

Trailers manufactured after 1 April 1980 must also be fitted with one rear red fog lamp.

Trailers manufactured after 1 October 1990 must be provided with two (non-triangular) white forward facing retro-reflectors.

Trailers manufactured after 1 October 1990 (and with a width – excluding load – of over 2.1 metres) must have:

  i 2 forward facing white end-outline marker lights,
  ii 2 rearward facing red end-outline marker lights (NB red and white lights on one side of a trailer may be combined into a single unit with a single light source). All trailers with a length exceeding 5 metres – excluding hitching device and any over-hanging load – must, additionally be fitted with at least 2 amber side facing retro-reflectors on each side of the trailer. If the trailer is longer, more will be mandatory.

Boat trailers do not normally require front position lights. However if they project more than 400 mm sideways from the illuminated area of the tow vehicle's front position light, that side must be fitted with a forward facing white light. If the load projects similarly, the load or trailer must be provided with a forward facing white light.

Overhanging loads and projections will also require the appropriate lighting in cases where they project more than 1 metre forward of the vehicle or rearward of the trailer. If the load projects rearwards more than 1 metre it must be lit by an additional rear light and a red retro-reflector not less than 1 metre from the end of the load. Usually it is possible to site the lighting board so as to comply with this requirement but care must be taken to ensure that a mast does not overhang too far.

Tyres

As with the tow car, it is illegal to mix radial and cross ply tyres on the same axle. Tyres must have the minimum tread decreed by current regulations and must be correctly inflated.

Number plate

This must be identical in shape, colour and type to that of the tow vehicle. At night it must be adequately lighted. It must be kept clear of mud and dirt.

The foregoing is a simplified summary of regulations affecting trailers and has not dealt with those of a size which would be towed by a goods vehicle. In all cases, safety on the road must be the prime consideration and it is the driver's responsibility to ensure that the trailed load is secure, that the weight does not exceed the capabilites of the tow vehicle (although for private cars there is, as yet no express stipulation) and that trailer and car are roadworthy. Failure to comply may result in prosecution.

Further information can be obtained from the Road Vehicles (Construction & Use) available from HMSO. As regulations may change slightly, not only as regards trailer construction and specifications but also in such matters as documentation, speed and motorway restrictions, readers are advised to seek advice from motoring organisations, especially before going foreign.

Also check for any particular requirements of ferry operators and the Channel Tunnel Shuttle as regulations affecting carriage of LPG cylinders, inboard and outboard motors (especially the fuel tanks and containers) may be subject to change.

It is most important to inform the insurers of both motor vehicle and boat of the intention to trail, both in this country and abroad and to ensure that adequate cover is arranged.

Index